Northwestern University
STUDIES IN *Phenomenology &*
Existential Philosophy

Consciousness and the
Acquisition of Language

Maurice Merleau-Ponty

Translated by

Consciousness and the Acquisition of Language

HUGH J. SILVERMAN

NORTHWESTERN UNIVERSITY PRESS

EVANSTON 1973

Northwestern University Press
Evanston, Illinois 60201

Originally published in French as "La Conscience et l'acquisition du language," *Bulletin de psychologie* no. 236, 18:3–6 (1964). English translation © 1973 by Northwestern University Press. First published 1973 by Northwestern University Press. First paperback edition published 1979. Third paperback printing, 1991. All rights reserved.

Printed in the United States of America

ISBN 0-8101-0597-7

The paper used in this publication meets the minimum requirements of American National Standard for Information Sciences—Permanence of Paper for Printed Library Materials, ANSI Z39.48-1984.

Contents

Foreword

NOT MANY PROFESSORS of philosophy in these parts would feel comfortable about letting the students enrolled in their courses take their words down stenographically and then publish them, with or without their formal approval. Much of the material which has come down to us from ancient and medieval philosophers is, on the contrary, in the form of *reportationes* of courses taken down by students. In letting so many of his courses [1] be published by his students before he himself was anywhere near ready to publish his own thoughts on these subjects in his own name and in his own style, Merleau-Ponty continued the hoary medieval traditions of the University of Paris. We who now have not only his own published works but also a large number of his courses can compare and contrast them with one another, and we are immediately struck by how clearly written, easy to understand, and analytically organized his courses were in contrast to his published books. Unlike the

---

1. A complete list of these courses and their chronological sequence is given in Hugh J. Silverman's Preface to this translation. Mr. Silverman's discussion of these published and unpublished courses is a most important contribution, particularly inasmuch as the two major bibliographies of Merleau-Ponty's works (namely, that to be found in Albert Rabil, *Merleau-Ponty, Existentialist of the Social World*, [New York: Columbia University Press, 1967], and that to be found in Richard L. Lanigan, "Maurice Merleau-Ponty Bibliography," *Man and World*, III, no. 1 [February, 1970]) make almost no mention of these courses.

Reportata Parisiensia of John Duns Scotus or the *logoi* of Aristotle, with their impenetrable obscurities (which we often blame on the fact that they are reworked lecture notes frequently composed by alien hands that have condensed, reordered, edited, and even editorialized on the ideas of the master), Merleau-Ponty's lectures are lucidity itself. Would that the arguments in the *Phenomenology of Perception* were as easy to follow!

This fact must give us pause. Clearly, a lot was said in these courses which has not been taken down. The strict outline of Merleau-Ponty's thought is emphasized, while the exuberant flora and fauna of his imagination, the deliberately ambiguous, intense, allusive character of his own prose style has been excised. With it have gone the nuances, qualifications, second-thoughts, dialectical twists, and reversals so characteristic of his method of argument as well. In reading this course of lectures we must, therefore, be ready to interpret and supply what is literally lacking but always subunderstood and to read what Merleau-Ponty says here in the light of all his other publications on the philosophy of language. There is much more behind each and every argument presented here in outline form than is supplied in this text itself, and we must caution the reader against thinking that an exclusive reading of this text alone will give a sufficiently complete account of his work on language. These lecture notes provide neither a comprehensive grasp of his thought as a whole nor a sound basis for its critical evaluation and possible refutation. In the very nature of the case these lecture notes are often extremely condensed: a sentence may serve to recall an argument; a few sentences may summarize for those who heard them in a determinate context a position which will appear opaque to us now.

But, having duly issued this caveat, this particular course, among all those we have, merits special attention and study. It marks a central step in Merleau-Ponty's development. While it is itself the culmination of a number of courses and preparatory studies which led up to it, it introduces themes which will be taken up one by one in later, more detailed studies. It presents us with the program for research in the philosophy of language which he was to prosecute from this time onward until his death.

The following remarks are meant to provide a sketch of the wider context of his thought on language within which this particular text should be read.

I. MERLEAU-PONTY'S EARLY PHILOSOPHY OF LANGUAGE

SHORTLY AFTER FINISHING the *Phenomenology of Perception,* which was published in 1945, Merleau-Ponty began reading scientific linguistics, particularly Saussure. This was also the period when he was writing *Humanism and Terror* and thinking of the problem of the philosophy of history. Saussure does not occur in the bibliography of either the *Phenomenology of Perception* or *The Structure of Behavior* and is not mentioned in the text of the celebrated chapter on "The Body as Expression and Speech," which appeared in the former work. Saussure's work is first used in the course on language which Merleau-Ponty gave at Lyon in 1947–48 and first becomes a central consideration in the text we are publishing here. We will take up Merleau-Ponty's interpretation of Saussure shortly; here let us focus our attention on the reason why Merleau-Ponty would find Saussure's theory of the linguistic "sign" so congenial.

In his chapter on "The Body as Expression and Speech" in the *Phenomenology of Perception,* it is clear that Merleau-Ponty's interest in language is limited to an investigation of the role that speech acts play in the bodily and perceptual constitution of our lived-world, of how the structures of speaking are related to, embedded in, and affect perception. He develops a "gestural" theory of expression. The body is expressive of meaning in many ways more fundamental than speaking; speaking is but the refinement, specification, and extension of preverbal behaviors which already bestow a human sense on the world. Our very motility and acts of bodily attention polarize our sensory faculties, select objects, and objectify reality; the selection of perceptual objects and the recognition of their affective tonalities is accomplished through sensory-motor behaviors which do not require the use of words. Moreover, the expression of our mental states in gestures, such as expressions of desire, frustration, concern, anger, pleasure, joy, etc., gives us the paradigm notion of what a "sign" is, namely, the physical embodiment and expression of a meaning which is strictly inseparable from its bodily expression. An expression of anger does not transmit a pure thought from one mind to another; like a mother's smile, which communicates an affective state which is immediately understood and responded to by the child—without concepts and without analogizing—the bodily expression of anger (or any other emotion) signifies itself. It *is* the physical appearance of meaning.

It was natural for Merleau-Ponty to extend this gestural notion of "sign" to the linguistic "word." He did this without reference to Saussure but later interprets himself as having anticipated what he would find in Saussure. Saussure defined a linguistic sign as the indissoluble unity of a meaning (*signifié*) with a physical sound or mark (*signifiant,* acoustic image). He wrote in one place:

> People have often compared the bilateral unity [of the physical aspect and the meaning aspect of linguistic signs] to the unity of the human person, composed of body and soul. This analogy is unsatisfactory. It would be more exact to think of a chemical compound, like water, which is a combination of hydrogen and oxygen. Taken separately, each of these elements has none of the properties of water.[2]

Whatever we may think of this odd analogy, it does serve to stress Saussure's belief that the physical expression of a meaning and the meaning expressed are inseparable, and that meaning cannot be found or investigated otherwise than through a study of the words in which it is fully incarnate. This is precisely Merleau-Ponty's position already in the *Phenomenology of Perception,* and it leads him into a rather paradoxical position.

He writes:

> . . . [it must] be recognized that the listener receives thought from speech itself. . . . People can speak to us only a language which

2. *Ferdinand de Saussure, Cours de linguistique générale,* 3d ed. (Paris: Payot, 1969), p. 145 (my translation). English translation by Wade Basken, *Course in General Linguistics* (New York: Philosophical Library, 1959), p. 103.

we already understand, each word of a difficult text awakens in us thoughts which were ours beforehand, but these meanings sometimes combine to form new thought which recasts them all, and we are transported to the heart of the matter, we find the source. Here there is nothing comparable to the solution of a problem, where we discover an unknown quantity through its relationship with known ones. For the problem can be solved only if it is determinate, that is, if the cross-checking of the data provides the unknown quantity with one or more definite values. In understanding others, the problem is always indeterminate because only the solution will bring the data retrospectively to light as convergent. . . . There is, then, a taking up of others' thought through speech . . . an ability to think *according to others*. . . . Here the meaning of words must be finally induced by the words themselves, or more exactly, their conceptual meaning must be formed by a kind of subtraction from a *gestural meaning*, which is immanent in speech.[3]

Merleau-Ponty then proceeds to endorse the ultimate consequences of this notion: the relation of the word-sound to *its* meaning cannot be purely "conventional."

If we consider only the conceptual and delimiting meaning of words, it is true that the verbal form . . . appears arbitrary. But it would no longer appear so if we took into account the emotional content of the word, which we have called above its "gestural" sense, which is all-important for poetry, for example. It would then be found that the words, vowels and phonemes are so many ways of "singing" the world, and that their function is to represent things not, as the naïve onomatopoeic theory had it, by reason of an objective resemblance, but because they extract, and literally express, their emotional essence. If it were possible, in any vocabulary, to disregard what is attributable to the mechanical laws of phonetics, to the influences of other languages, the rationalization of grammarians, the assimilatory processes, we should probably discover in the original form of each language a somewhat restricted system of expression, but such as would make it not entirely arbitrary to call night by the word *nuit* if we use *lumière* for light. The predominance of vowels in one language, or of consonants in another, and constructional and syntactical systems, do not represent so many arbitrary conventions for the expression

3. Maurice Merleau-Ponty, *Phenomenology of Perception*, trans. Colin Smith (New York: The Humanities Press, 1962) pp. 178–79 (translation corrected).

of one and the same idea, but several ways for the human body to sing the world's praises and in the last resort to live it. Hence the *full* meaning of a language is never translatable into another. We may speak several languages, but one of them always remains the one in which we live. In order completely to assimilate a language, it would be necessary to make the world which it expresses one's own, and one never does belong to two worlds at once. . . . Strictly speaking, therefore, there are no conventional signs . . .[4]

If we are properly attuned to the dialectical cast of his thought and style, it is not necessary to attempt an empirical validation or refutation of this statement by examining cases of bilingualism and the like.[5] As usual, Merleau-Ponty is bringing into the clearest opposition possible two theoretically defensible viewpoints on the phenomenon of language neither of which is *exclusively* true: namely, that different languages can speak of the *same things* in different phonemic patterns, following different phonological rules, while at the same time there remains beneath the level of what these patterned sounds enable one to think conceptually, an untranslatable, primitive level of meaning distinctive of that language and expressive of its primordial melody, intonation, and poetic "chant." And it is the latter fact that is, at least chronologically and existentially, prior to the former. For the speakers of a given language, for the child learning the language, and for the mature speaker or writer using it to express what has not before been said, the pairing of meanings with word-sounds is accomplished by "an unknown law" that enables us to make use of our bodies and their natural powers of vocal gesticulation for purposes that transcend them, namely, to mean, express, and understand the world as humanly comprehensible, as the intended correlate of behaviors that themselves "make sense," and to confer a sense on the objects that polarize them. In this, every language is equally "natural" and equally conventional; it is natural to man to speak, but no particular use of his speech apparatus, no particular "natural" language, is in-

4. *Ibid.*, pp. 187–88 (translation corrected).
5. Cf. my article "Was Merleau-Ponty a Structuralist?," *Semiotica*, IV, no. 4 (1971), 309–11.

scribed in human nature. It is as "natural" for man to "sing the world" in Japanese as in English.

> The psycho-physiological equipment leaves a great variety of possibilities open, and there is no more here than in the realm of instinct a human nature finally and immutably given. The use a man is to make of his body is transcendent in relation to that body as a mere biological entity. It is no more natural, and no less conventional, to shout in anger or to kiss in love than to call a table a "table." [6]

Thus, we find in Merleau-Ponty's earliest writings on language two doctrines which he later finds in Saussure. *The first* is the definition of a "sign" as the indissoluble unity which binds meaning to *its* word(s)—a thesis which leads Merleau-Ponty to deny the possibility of an eidetic, universal, apriori grammar.

The second is the closely related discovery of a level of meaning in speech which is more fundamental and more primitive than that of the translatable conceptual thought with which philosophers usually are exclusively concerned. Merleau-Ponty is a philosopher of language who is concerned primarily with the primitive phonemic processes which terminate in the production of *words*.[7] He never really goes beyond the consideration of words to the questions of syntax which, for Husserl no less than for the logical grammarians, are primary.

Merleau-Ponty's attitude toward language is quite idiosyncratic for a philosopher and, in this, he is extremely original. He discovers and pays special attention to what no philosopher from Plato on down ever had any interest in, namely, the kind of meaning which exists just on the level of the phonemic patterns that are capable of being accepted (given the natural phonology of that given language) by that language's native speakers. He calls attention to, and orchestrates, the primordial melody, intonation, and musical contour which characterize the babbling of children as they are learning their first words, the kind of babbling that in children of around two years of age results in their first true speech. The newborn infant, during its first twelve to eighteen

---

6. Merleau-Ponty, *Phenomenology of Perception*, p. 189.

7. Cf. my article, "The Present Status of the Phenomenology of Language," to be published by Duquesne University Press in the Proceedings of the Fifth Lexington Conference, ed. Erwin Straus.

months (or thereabouts), produces in endless profusion all the myriad sounds which the natural vocal apparatus is capable of producing—randomly, without selection, without sense. Then, as the child begins to react with its environment on a more sophisticated level, it begins little by little, and sometimes more or less suddenly, to restrict the sounds it is capable of producing to closer and closer approximations of those sounds actually being spoken in its linguistic environment. The German child begins to babble with a German accent, the English child begins to babble according to the pattern of his native language until, little by little, he restricts the number of sounds he is even capable of uttering and recognizing to just those which are recognized in just that particular linguistic community. By this time he has internalized, without conceptualization, the phonological system of his native language.

Now, the point here is that these natural signs, employed as phonemes according to strict phonological laws, do not *in themselves mean anything* other than themselves; it is their combinations, according to phonological rules, which enable the speaker to form *words* which *do* mean something, in that they refer beyond themselves to things, events, and contexts of real, nonverbal experience. But, Merleau-Ponty's first point is that words, even when they finally achieve the ability to carry referential and, eventually, conceptual levels of meaning, never completely lose that primitive, strictly phonemic, level of "affective" meaning which is not translatable into their conceptual definitions. There is, he argues, an affective tonality, a mode of conveying meaning beneath the level of thought, beneath the level of the words themselves (which the phonological patterns permit to come into existence), which is contained in the words *just insofar as they are patterned sounds,* as just the sounds which this particular historical language uniquely uses, and which are much more like a melody—a "singing of the world"—than fully translatable, conceptual thought. Merleau-Ponty is almost alone among philosophers of language in his sensitivity to this level of meaning. It is a level of affective communication which seems to belong to processes that, in themselves, are nonverbal but are a necessary part of the formation and production of words.

II. The Turning Point: Structuralism

It is interesting to note that, later on, after reading Saussure, Merleau-Ponty credits the discovery of this primitive level of phonemic meaning "whose very existence intellectualism does not suspect"[8] not to himself exclusively, but to Saussure as well.[9] The turning point seems to have occurred about the time of the publication of this course on *Consciousness and the Acquisition of Language*. For a few years his expression of discipleship to Saussure is total. From 1949 onward his writings on language multiply rapidly. Language begins to become his central preoccupation; it is no longer treated as just one example among many of the specifically human institutions of meaning, but now becomes the privileged model of the whole of our experience of meaning. From being a peripheral, though always essential, consideration in his phenomenological program, the analysis of language now begins to take central place. In 1951, in a paper which he read at the first *Colloque international de phénoménologie,* he attributes his own preoccupation to Husserl as well:

> Precisely because the problem of language does not, in the philosophical tradition, belong to first philosophy, Husserl treats it much more freely than the problems of perception or of knowledge. *He puts it in the central position,* and the little he says of it is original and enigmatic. This problem, therefore, permits us better than any other to question phenomenology and not only to repeat Husserl but to continue his work, to take up again the movement of his thought rather than to repeat his doctrines.[10]

This attempt to present phenomenology as a generalized theory of language grows stronger in Merleau-Ponty's later

8. Merleau-Ponty, *Phenomenology of Perception,* p. 179.

9. Maurice Merleau-Ponty, *La Prose du monde,* ed. Claude Lefort (Paris: Gallimard, 1969, pp. 45, 161. English translation by John O'Neill, *The Prose of the World* (Evanston, Ill.: Northwestern University Press, 1973), pp. 31, 115.

10. These are the first lines of Merleau-Ponty's famous article "On the Phenomenology of Language," which is included in *Signs,* trans. Richard C. McCleary (Evanston, Ill.: Northwestern University Press, 1964), p. 84. This is, however, my own translation of Merleau-Ponty's words; emphasis added.

writings, and in this he can clearly be seen as a precursor of present-day structuralism. Moreover, in his Inaugural Address to the Collège de France in 1953 he went so far as to credit Saussurian linguistics with developing a "theory of signs" that could serve as a sounder basis for the philosophy of history than the thought of either Marx or Hegel.[11] He did not, perhaps, believe (like the later Wittgenstein) that the study of language would solve all philosophical problems, but he did believe that linguistics would give us the paradigm model on the basis of which we would be able to elaborate a theory of the human sciences and thus establish a universal, philosophical anthropology.

Whether either Husserl or Saussure deserves the roles which Merleau-Ponty gives them in the writings of this period is something which will be endlessly discussed. Our final judgment is rendered the more difficult in that Merleau-Ponty never completed the work he began along these lines. Most of his "linguistic" and "structuralist" essays fall in the years 1949–59.[12] By the time of

11. Maurice Merleau-Ponty, *In Praise of Philosophy*, trans. James M. Edie and John Wild (Evanston, Ill.: Northwestern University Press, 1963), pp. 54–55. These statements in Merleau-Ponty's inaugural address of 1953 are in striking contrast with his earlier statements in *Humanism and Terror*, trans. John O'Neill (Boston: Beacon Press, 1969) and in an essay written in 1946, "The Yogi and the Proletarian," that Marxism is not just one philosophy of history but is *the* philosophy of history. Cf. *Humanism and Terror*, p. 153. Merleau-Ponty's development toward structuralism in the period between this essay (1946) and his course on *Consciousness and the Acquisition of Language* (1949) brought about a profound development and reinterpretation of his early work, a reinterpretation which has not been sufficiently noted by his commentators.

12. The most important of these essays are the following:

(1) *Langage et communication* [1948], Cours de l'Université de Lyon, 1948, unpublished. See Preface.

(2) *Consciousness and the Acquisition of Language* [1949]. See Preface.

(3) "Phenomenology and the Sciences of Man" [1951]. English translation by John Wild, in *The Primacy of Perception and Other Essays*, ed. James M. Edie (Evanston, Ill.: Northwestern University Press, 1964) pp. 43–95.

(4) "On the Phenomenology of Language" [1951]. English translation in *Signs*, pp. 84–97.

(5) "The Philosopher and Sociology" [1951]. English translation in *Signs*, pp. 98–113.

his candidacy for a professorship of philosophy at the Collège de France, he had already half completed his work on what was to be his major, comprehensive treatise on the philosophy of language, *La Prose du monde*. But after 1952–53 he seems, little by little, to have lost interest in this particular work, and he definitively abandoned it altogether after 1959.[13] *La Prose du monde*, which was posthumously edited by Claude Lefort in 1969, must then be dated as roughly contemporaneous with Merleau-Ponty's assuming his chair at the Collège de France, therefore at the highwater mark of his Saussurian enthusiasm and his new interest in structural linguistics.

After 1959, when he abandoned this particular work, he seems to have put together a whole series of interim working manuscripts (entitled variously "L'Origine de la vérité," "Généalogie du vrai," and "Être et monde") under the new title, *The Visible and the Invisible*, the book he was working on at the time of his death and which we now possess in the posthumous form

---

(6) "Indirect Language and the Voices of Silence," [1952]. English translation in *Signs*, pp. 39–83.

(7) "An Unpublished Text by Maurice Merleau-Ponty: A Prospectus of His Work" [1953]. English translation in *Primacy of Perception*, pp. 3–11. This is the prospectus of his work which Merleau-Ponty presented to the Collège de France as a candidate for a professorship of philosophy there; it gives a historical outline of the development of his thought and shows how he himself interpreted his growing interest in language, and the place of his philosophy of language in his work as a whole.

(8) *In Praise of Philosophy* [1953], his inaugural address at the Collège de France.

(9) "The Sensible World and the World of Expression" [1953], his first course at the Collège de France. English translation in *Themes from the Lectures at the Collège de France, 1952–1960*, trans. John O'Neill (Evanston, Ill.: Northwestern University Press, 1970), pp. 3–11.

(10) "Studies in the Literary Use of Language" [1953]. English trans. in *ibid.*, pp. 12–18.

(11) "The Problem of Speech" [1954]. English trans. in *ibid.*, pp. 19–26.

(12) "From Mauss to Claude Lévi-Strauss" [1959]. English trans. in *Signs*, pp. 114–25.

13. See the "Avertissement" by Claude Lefort to *La Prose du monde*, pp. i, ix–xi. English translation, pp. xi–xii, xvii–xix.

of a half-completed treatise followed by an intriguing but unfinished mass of "working notes." [14]

It is not to the point here to analyze or repeat the historical development of Merleau-Ponty's philosophy of language in complete detail. It is sufficient to indicate the direction his thought was taking as he was working out his most mature conception of the place of the philosophy of language in his systematic phenomenology of the experienced world.

His starting point was Saussure's theory of the linguistic sign:

> We have learned from Saussure that, taken singly, signs do not signify anything, and that each one of them does not so much express a meaning as mark a divergence of meaning between itself and other signs. [15]

> The well-known definition of the sign as "diacritical, oppositive, and negative" means that language is present in the speaking subject as a system of intervals between signs and significations, and that, as a unity, the act of speech simultaneously operates the differentiation of these two orders. [16]

In the papers he published during the period just before and just after he assumed his chair at the Collège de France, he elaborated a theory of the relationship of language and speech to "silence." In order to understand what Merleau-Ponty means by the "silence" which surrounds language and enables language *to occur as speech,* we must recognize the distinction between *la langue* and *la parole* which he was elaborating at this time. [17] On the one hand speech acts, exercises of *la parole,* institute *la langue* and make it live, but on the other hand speech itself is possible only on the background of all the subunderstood phonological, morphological, and syntactical rules, as well as within the

14. *Ibid.,* p. xi. *Le Visible et l'invisible* was edited posthumously by Claude Lefort (Paris: Gallimard, 1964). English translation by Alphonso Lingis (Evanston, Ill.: Northwestern University Press, 1968).

15. *Signs,* p. 117.

16. *Themes from the Lectures,* pp. 19–20.

17. I have dealt with these points in more detail in my article on "The Significance of Merleau-Ponty's Philosophy of Language," which will appear in the near future in the *Journal of the History of Philosophy.*

context of the particular lexicon, of our *langue*. We use *la langue* in the way we use our bodies, without thought and without explicit consciousness of the structures which we are bringing into action at any one point. The first meaning of the "silence" which makes speech possible is that of *la langue,* which itself does not speak but is the *ground* of all speech; this "silence" is not unstructured—it is highly determinate. Moreover, and this is even more important in our actual acts of speaking, the speech acts of *la parole* (our particular usages of our common language in each particular case) result in a kind of "coherent deformation" of the already sedimented meanings and intentions which form the silent background for our speech and which is constituted of all the forms, all the linguistic institutions of the historical tradition of our distinctive linguistic culture. We speak, in short, on the background of a complex, determinate, and already articulated matrix of linguistic structures which at each instant enables our speech acts to take place, and thus enables us to break silence and to say something new in authentic and original acts of meaning. Thus, *la parole* brings about a constant dislocation and continuing change in *la langue*. We may use the same words as we have used on previous occasions, or as the great thinkers and philosophers, the classical writers of our literary tradition, have used, but the meaning of these words is never fully grasped and transmitted once and for all. The very *meaning* of our words is itself a limit-concept which eludes speech by always escaping beyond it into the transcendental silence of the realm of conceptual thought, and which, while polarizing our attempts at expression, always escapes us to some extent, and thus always leaves room for more to be said, for our *langue* to be used by countless other speakers and writers for *their* purposes and for *their* intentions, which will, in turn, introduce us into *new* realms of linguistic meaning which are nevertheless comprehensible and communicable to all on the basis of a common understanding and acceptance of *this* language, an acceptance of common rules which is *sufficient* for all purposes of communication but which is never fully *adequate* to bring any particular expression to completion.

Unfortunately, these fascinating approaches to a generalized theory of language, which we find in the various specialized essays published between 1949–59, were never systematically unified or finished. Instead, after 1959, Merleau-Ponty sought more and more to bring together all of his earlier insights concerning language into a final theory which would give us a "new conception of reason" [18] by showing us the proper way to understand the reciprocal "founding" of reason and perception and thus to see how language and the world analogize one another.

In the final pages of *The Visible and the Invisible* [19] Merleau-Ponty attempts to show that the human body, as a system of structured possibilities for future action (which are realized in the "objectification" and in the very discovery of perceptual objects) is "structured like language." Language, as he saw it, following Saussure, is a "diacritical, relative, oppositional system" of elements which are not "absolute" bits of meaning but rather only "divergencies" (*écarts*) sufficient to enable us to establish a system of linguistic signs or *words* (in which all the phonological, morphological, and syntactical structures of our language terminate—since, after all, language is constituted only of *words*) which themselves have meaning for us only because they are opposable, according to rule, to all the other linguistic signs (or words), of the same category and level, which our language permits.

It is the task of the philosopher of language, ultimately, to show how linguistic structures mirror and analogize the structures of perception, enable us to understand the structures of action which give us our primordial motives for distinguishing any one object, and any aspect of any object, from any other, and thus produce, emanating from the active subject (as an embodied consciousness), the actual lived-world of our perceptual experience.

Just as we say that it is *a part of the meaning* of a color adjective in the English language (such as, for instance, "red" or "brown"), that *any other* color adjective, recognized and discriminated in the lexicon of that language, *could* (from the point

---

18. *La Prose du monde*, pp. 34 ff. English translation, p. 23.
19. These are the "final pages" that we have; they were not the end he himself planned for this uncompleted book.

of view of purely formal syntactical analysis) take its place, according to rule, in a given linguistic string, so Merleau-Ponty wants to say that colors themselves, as perceived, are not so much "things" as "a difference between things." Let me refer briefly to his analysis of the perception of the color "red":

> A punctuation in the field of red things, which includes the tiles of roof tops, the flags of gatekeepers and of the Revolution, certain terrains near Aix or in Madagascar, it is also a punctuation in the field of red garments, which includes, along with the dresses of women, robes of professors, bishops, and advocate generals, and also in the field of adornments and that of uniforms. And its red literally is not the same as it appears in one constellation or in the other, as the pure essence of the Revolution of 1917 precipitates in it, or that of the eternal feminine, or that of the public prosecutor, or that of the gypsies dressed like hussars who reigned twenty-five years ago over an inn on the Champs-Elysées. A certain red is also a fossil drawn up from the depths of imaginary worlds. If we took all these participations into account we would recognize that a naked color, and in general a visible, is not a chunk of absolutely hard, indivisible being, offered all naked to a vision which could be only total or null, but is rather a sort of straits between exterior horizons and interior horizons ever gaping open, something that comes to touch lightly and makes diverse regions of the colored or visible world resound at the distances, a certain differentiation, an ephemeral modulation of this world—*less a color or a thing, therefore, than a difference between things and colors.*[20]

One conclusion of this analysis would be that the *ideality* which philosophers of language attribute to *the word* is mirrored in the ideality (or "invisibility," in one of the many imperfectly distinguished senses which Merleau-Ponty gives to this term) of what words themselves *refer to*. There simply is, he seems to be saying, no such thing as an experience of "red" itself; every experience is of a "particular red thing" which is opposable to every other (qualitatively distinguishable) instance of what we would be disposed to take (for cultural reasons we hardly understand) as another "red" thing. In short, the experience of "red" (and of any other color) is always the experience of an instance or an example of "red" and thus always implies the subunderstood rules which determine what is to count for us as an example of "red"

20. *The Visible and the Invisible,* pp. 131–33 (emphasis added).

and what is to be rejected as being "of another color." However fine the discriminations of the color adjectives of our natural language, or of our private idiolect of that language, we will never escape the component of ideality involved in our (cultural and intersubjectively determined) selective, perceptual perceiving of colors.

In short, the structures of perception are, for Merleau-Ponty, strict analogues of the structures of language. Colors are as "ideal" as phonemes: that is, the actual experiences of what we call red objects are to the color "red" what raw phonetics is to the ideal laws of phonemics. The phonemes (and the syntagmatic and paradigmatic rules for their opposability) which constitute the phonological system of any given natural language are, *strictly as phonemes,* not sounds at all. They are not the raw phonetic material which given historical speakers actually produce; they are, in fact, *never actually spoken, but only meant.* That a similar structure of diacritical, relative, oppositional rules governs perception, and all other forms of objectification, was Merleau-Ponty's final belief and underlies his final and most mature attempt to relate the various orders of intentionality to one another.

III. Consciousness and the Acquisition of Language

Perhaps the best way, then, to interpret the text we are publishing here is to bear in mind that it stands at the origin of Merleau-Ponty's later philosophy of language; it states in their first and original form all of the themes concerning language which Merleau-Ponty developed in his later corpus and, in fact, serves the purpose of a general introduction to all his later writings on the philosophy of language.

It does not present great difficulties of interpretation, once its context has been made clear, and I will therefore put my final remarks schematically under two headings, namely (1) Merleau-Ponty's argument against the possibility of a universal logical grammar and (2) his specific theory of the speech act.

(1) We have seen above (p. xix) that Merleau-Ponty ap-

proves of and follows Husserl's decision to put the theory of lan guage at the center of his philosophical investigations and that he finds "the little" Husserl had to say on the subject to be "original and enigmatic." What Merleau-Ponty finds especially "enigmatic" is the whole of the *Fourth Investigation* and most of *Formal and Transcendental Logic*—hardly a minor chunk of Husserl—particularly because of its theory of pure apriori grammar. In his essays "On the Phenomenology of Language" [21] and "Phenomenology and the Sciences of Man," [22] as well as in this course on *Consciousness and the Acquisition of Language,* he attempts to interpret Husserl, unhistorically, in his own sense and even seems to think that Husserl later abandoned his idea of a universal logical grammar.[23] Against traditional logical grammarians (and against such recent developments as Chomskyan transformational grammar had he known them), Merleau-Ponty frequently and explicitly tries to rule out the possibility of linguistic universals. He does this primarily for two reasons.[24]

He seems to believe, first of all, that to investigate language from this universalistic, eidetic point of view necessitates a return to the discredited attempt of Carnap and the logical positivists to replace natural languages with an "ideal language"—a task which might be of interest for logicians but which cannot, because of this very restriction, tell us anything philosophically significant about "natural language"—in which alone he is interested.

The second and more important reason is that his own gestural theory of meaning makes it necessary that no natural language be the exact equivalent of any other—either in its actual

---

21. *Signs,* pp. 84 ff.

22. *The Primacy of Perception,* pp. 78 ff. (in the section on "Linguistics").

23. Cf. my article, "Husserl's Conception of 'The Grammatical' and Contemporary Linguistics," in *Life-World and Consciousness,* ed. Lester E. Embree (Evanston, Ill.: Northwestern University Press, 1972), pp. 259 ff.

24. These reasons, enlarged to three, are developed in much greater detail in my article, "Can Grammar Be Thought?," in *Patterns of the Life-World,* ed. James M. Edie, Francis H. Parker, Calvin O. Schrag (Evanston, Ill.: Northwestern University Press, 1970), pp. 322 ff.

form or in its potentialities for expression. His arguments for this position seem strongest when he is developing his fundamental "phonemic" theory of meaning; they appear to get weaker whenever we turn from the level of "words" (with which he is exclusively concerned) to the higher levels of syntax, where purely formal laws seem to hold. Though he occasionally recognized an "algorithmic" aspect to language (and gives this considerably more space in *La Prose du monde* than in any of his other writings), he has no theory which permits him to distinguish depth from surface linguistic structures and thus to account adequately for the purely formal aspects of grammar. Nevertheless, we note in all these texts that he does not so much flatly deny any "universal categories" as state somewhat more hesitantly: "the possibility of a universal grammar remains problematic" (p. 88 below). Elsewhere he uses such locutions as: "if universality is to be attained," [25] "if there is such a thing as universal thought," [26] "but even if these invariants exist," [27] rather than outright, conclusive denial. The reason for this is that he is himself committed to the kind of "existential" universality involved in his "presumption" that all kinds of texts *can* be deciphered, that all human cultures *can* be understood, and that all men *can* communicate with one another.[28]

The only foundation for universality that Merleau-Ponty will accept is not the "eidetic" universality of a necessary apriori logical form but the comprehensibility achieved in "the oblique passage from a given language that I speak . . . to another given language that I learn." [29] The event is too hesitant and passing to imagine that some common mind or some explicit convention is responsible for it; at the same time it is too systematic, too consistent to be reducible to a series of accidents. On the one hand there is the practical impossibility of giving *one*, ideal, formal analysis of any given language which would explicitly show forth its unique logical form and thus enable us to define its essential

25. *Signs*, p. 87.
26. *Phenomenology of Perception*, p. 188.
27. *Signs*, p. 119.
28. Cf. "Was Merleau-Ponty a Structuralist?," pp. 319–20.
29. *Signs*, p. 87.

structure unequivocally by deriving all its various substructures from a common principle that shows their proper hierarchies and derivations. It is equally impossible to account rationally for the historical relationships between languages or to pinpoint the time, for example, at which Latin irrevocably becomes French. But, at the same time, when one takes up the linguistic history of the human race, the continuous proliferation of aberrant forms in which no structure is ever fully finished or achieved, and in which no innovation can be precisely dated, one sees that there is no precise break between any one language and any other, no clean line of demarcation between one dialect and another. At this point, says Merleau-Ponty, one sees that "to be precise, *there is only one language in a state of becoming.*" [30]

> If we must renounce the abstract universality of a rational grammar which would give us the common essence of all languages, we rediscover at the same time the concrete universality of a given language which is becoming different from itself while remaining the same. Because I am now speaking, my language is not for me a sum of facts but a unified instrument for a complete intention of expression. And *because it is so for me I am able to enter into other systems of expression,* at first by grasping them as variants of my own, and then by letting myself be inhabited by them until my own language becomes a variant of them. Neither the unity of language, nor the distinctions among languages, nor their historical derivations from one another cease to be understandable just because we refuse to conceive one essence of language. It is simply that they must be conceived not from the standpoint of the concept or of essence but from the dimension of existence. [31]

There is, therefore, an experienced and "existential" foundation for universality in language, but it is not that of the "innate ideas" of the Cartesians or of the logical aprioris of "rational grammar." It is rather the "oblique" or "lateral" universality of incomplete but sufficient comprehensibility which we effect in actually speaking to others. We must each speak according to common rules or we would not be understood, and yet each act of speech is, in each case, a "coherent deformation" of the rules

30. *La Prose du monde,* p. 56. English translation, p. 39 (translation slightly altered).
31. *Ibid.* (my translation). English translation, pp. 39–40.

already given and accepted. In his essay on Lévi-Strauss Merleau-Ponty applies the same conception to social structures.

> There thus appears at the base of social systems a formal infrastructure (one is tempted to say an unconscious thought), an anticipation of the human mind, as if our science were already completed in events, and the human order of culture a second order of nature dominated by other invariants. But even if these invariants exist, even if social science were to find beneath structures a metastructure to which they conformed (as phonology does beneath phonemes), the universal we would thus arrive at could no more be substituted for the particular than general geometry annuls the local truth of Euclidean spatial relations. . . . The implications of a formal structure may well bring out the internal necessity of a given genetic sequence. *But it is not these implications which make men, society, and history exist.* . . . This process of joining objective analysis to lived experience is perhaps the most proper task of anthropology. . . . This provides *a second way to the universal:* no longer the overarching universal of a strictly objective method, but a sort of *lateral universal* which we acquire through ethnological experience and its incessant testing of the self through the other person and the other person through the self.[32]

(2) The second great achievement—and equally great paradox—in Merleau-Ponty's philosophy of language is his own peculiar version of the speech act (*la parole*). He was one of the first to turn philosophical attention to natural languages as such and (like the later Wittgenstein) to found his theory of language on the speech act, the act of actual usage as such (see pp. 31, 52, 60–61, 95 below). However, in so doing, he interprets Saussure in an enigmatic manner by stating that Saussure gave primacy to *la parole* over *la langue* in his study of language and by claiming in his paper "On the Phenomenology of Language" that Saussure distinguished "a synchronic linguistics of speech" from "a diachronic linguistics of language." [33] The fact of the matter is that, for Saussure, both synchrony and diachrony are aspects of *la langue*, whereas the study of what Merleau-Ponty calls *la parole*, the speech act as such, falls wholly outside the scientific

---

32. *Signs*, pp. 118–20 (emphasis added).
33. *Signs*, p. 86.

approach to language defined in Saussure's structural linguistics.[34]

Rather than distinguishing and opposing the formal, structural aspects of language as an ideal system to the actual acts of usage in which they are employed, Merleau-Ponty argues (in his essay "On the Phenomenology of Language" and elsewhere) that the "diachronic linguistics of language" can be absorbed in a "synchronic linguistics of speech" and that it is the latter which generates the former in such a way that there seems to be a total ontological dependence of *la langue* on *la parole*. Paul Ricoeur, for one, believes that this manner of approaching the ideal linguistic structure formalized by the scientific linguist makes any dialogue between Merleau-Ponty (or his followers) and modern linguistics impossible.[35] By claiming that the ideal system (*la langue*) is only an accident or by-product of the subjectively experienced acts of speakers, Ricoeur argues, Merleau-Ponty does not take the formal, algorithmic aspect of language, which he otherwise recognizes, with sufficient seriousness.

> The fact that the notion of language, taken as an autonomous system, is not given consideration weighs heavily on this phenomenology of the speech act. Its recourse to processes of "sedimentation" puts it back beside the old psychological notion of *habit*, an acquired ability, and thus the structural aspect as such is lost.[36]

In order to avoid the kind of psychologism which seems to be lurking here (and which, one might add, seems also to infect a number of contemporary post-Wittgensteinian theories of the speech act), what Merleau-Ponty has to show is how historical acts of speech taking place in individuals organized into a linguistic community not only generate understanding and make

34. Maurice Lagueux, "Merleau-Ponty et la linguistique de Saussure," *Dialogue* (1965), pp. 351–64, gives a sound statement of Merleau-Ponty's misreading of Saussure. I have tried to explain this undoubted distortion of Saussure's texts in a manner more favorable to Merleau-Ponty in "Was Merleau-Ponty a Structuralist?," pp. 304–5.

35. Paul Ricoeur, *Le Conflit des interpretations* (Paris: Seuil, 1969), pp. 244 ff.

36. *Ibid.*, p. 245.

communication possible but also generate that series of formal constraints which we call the laws of phonology, morphology, and syntax, and which seem, in the scientific study of language, to be logically prior to speech acts, i.e., to constitute the necessary formal framework within which phonemes, morphemes, words, and sentences can be built up. Certainly such objective laws are psychologically opaque; very few native speakers *know* (on a thematic level, i.e., as being able to state them explicitly) *what* the laws of linguistic usage accepted in their linguistic community *are*, even though they are able to produce, effortlessly, grammatical sentences and reject ungrammatical sentences *according to* these very rules. In short, the question which we are forced to address to Merleau-Ponty is whether his theory of language, which seems to be exclusively concerned with *words* as they occur in concrete acts of usage, does justice to the role of syntax in the production of meaning and, secondly, what the relation of syntax (if it is given a status independent of *la parole*) is to speech acts.[37]

To address such a question to Merleau-Ponty is, of course, not to imply that no answer can be given from within the resources of his own thought. It is precisely because his own theory is still unfinished but sufficiently determinate and sufficiently suggestive to tempt us to work out its implications that his philosophy of language is still of the greatest contemporary interest.

JAMES M. EDIE

Northwestern University
May, 1973

37. I believe that the only important attempt up to now to develop Merleau-Ponty's theory of the speech act further than he himself did occurs in: Paul Ricoeur, "La Structure, le mot, l'événement," first published in *Esprit* (May, 1967), and republished in *Man and World*, I, no. 1 (February, 1968), pp. 10–30, and in *Philosophy Today* (Summer, 1968), pp. 114–29. I have taken up some of the themes found in Ricoeur's work in my essay on "The Levels and Objectivity of Meaning," in *The Future of Metaphysics*, ed. Robert E. Wood (Chicago: Quadrangle Books, 1970), pp. 121–49.

Translator's Preface

IN THE YEAR 1949–50, Maurice Merleau-Ponty gave a course at the University of Paris entitled *La Conscience et l'acquisition du langage* (*Consciousness and the Acquisition of Language*). This course was held on Thursdays at 5 o'clock in the Guizot Amphitheater of the Sorbonne. He also taught two other courses on the same day: *Structure et conflits de la conscience enfantine* (*Structure and Conflicts in the Child's Consciousness*) at 3 o'clock and *L'Enfant vu par l'adulte* (*The Child as Seen by the Adult*) at 11 o'clock in the morning. The latter two series of lectures were basic requirements for the "Diplôme de Psychologie Pédagogique." All three courses could be taken by those studying for the "Licence de Psychologie."

The lecture notes taken down by students were periodically gathered together and submitted to Merleau-Ponty for his approval. Then every two or three weeks these notes were published in the *Bulletin du Groupe d'études de psychologie de l'Université de Paris*.[1] By the end of the year, one would have the full set of lectures as transcribed by students and as reviewed by Merleau-Ponty. Thus the volume of issues for 1949–50 contains the complete text of *Structure et conflits de la conscience enfantine*, of *L'Enfant vu par l'adulte*, and of *La Conscience et l'acquisition du langage*.

1. In 1940–50, this journal was only in its third volume. It still continues today as then under the direction of D. Voutsinas, although it is now entitled simply the *Bulletin de psychologie*.

The same procedure was followed for the lectures that Merleau-Ponty gave in 1950–51. The titles for this second year were: *Psycho-sociologie de l'enfant* (*Psychosociology of the Child*), *Les Relations avec autrui chez l'enfant* (*The Child's Relations with Others*), and *Les Sciences de l'homme et la phénoménologie* (*Phenomenology and the Sciences of Man*). Versions of *The Child's Relations with Others*, translated by William Cobb, and *Phenomenology and the Sciences of Man*, translated by John Wild, have been included by James M. Edie in *The Primacy of Perception*.[2] These translations, however, were based on the course material published by the Centre de documentation universitaire and not on the text ultimately published in the *Bulletin de psychologie*.[3]

In 1951–52, the lectures on *Phenomenology and the Sciences of Man* were completed, along with two new courses entitled: *Méthodes en psychologie de l'enfant* (*Methods in Child Psychology*) and *L'Expérience d'autrui* (*The Experience of Others*).

Merleau-Ponty taught at the University of Paris for only three years (from 1949–52). He was then elected to a chair in philosophy at the Collège de France in 1953, where he lectured until his death in 1961. In November, 1964, the *Bulletin de psychologie* gathered together into one volume all of Merleau-Ponty's courses, except the one on *L'Expérience d'autrui*. These were the same texts which had been published serially by the journal at the time that the courses were given. More recent printings of this volume have simply corrected some of the typographical errors of the original text. The reader of this translation will, however, find several translator's notes where I have indicated certain probable inaccuracies that remain in the most recently published French version.

It was the express wish of Madame Merleau-Ponty, as conveyed to me by Claude Lefort, that the nature of *Consciousness and the Acquisition of Language* be indicated to the reader. This course was not a carefully worked out or formally written book

2. Maurice Merleau-Ponty, *The Primacy of Perception*, ed. James M. Edie (Evanston, Ill.: Northwestern University Press, 1964).
3. *Bulletin de psychologie*, no. 236, XVIII 3–6 (1964).

on the order of *The Structure of Behavior* or *Phenomenology of Perception*.[4] Rather, it was a series of weekly lectures, transcribed by students and then approved by Merleau-Ponty himself.

To further emphasize the fact that this was a course, the *Bulletin du Groupe d'études de psychologie de l'Université de Paris* also included in its third volume various assignments that students were to submit to Merleau-Ponty. For example, there were three suggested topics for papers to be written by students taking the course on *Consciousness and the Acquisition of Language:* (1) The Child and the Animal; (2) Clinical Method in Child Psychology; and (3) Magical Elements of Child Consciousness.

In Volume IV, we find the following suggestion to students taking the course in 1950–51: "It would be very helpful to have reviewed and studied the courses offered by Professor Merleau-Ponty in 1949–50." In the same issue, there is a statement clarifying the nature of the examination for the Certificate in Child Psychology and Pedagogy:

> For the written examination in child psychology, M. Merleau-Ponty would like to specify that candidates should acquire a knowledge of the material on:
> (1) The Binet-Simon Test (with adjustments)
> (2) The Terman Test
> (3) The Grace Arthur Scale
> (4) The Rorschach Test
> (5) Drawings, writing, and play technique in the exploration of child behavior
> Note: In all cases, it will not suffice to know only the theory. Candidates must be able, for example, to interpret the results of a Rorschach plate, or be able to analyze a drawing.[5]

This latter point is significant if we remember that Merleau-Ponty is considered principally as a philosopher. When he

4. Maurice Merleau-Ponty, *The Structure of Behavior,* trans. Alden L. Fisher (Boston: Beacon Press, 1963); *Phenomenology of Perception,* trans. Colin Smith (London: Routledge & Kegan Paul, 1962).

5. It is common in American psychology for students to be aware of techniques, yet not understand the theory or history underlying the operations. In France, the reverse is more likely to occur.

accepted his appointment as Professor of Child Psychology and Pedagogy at the Institut de Psychologie, he had already published *The Structure of Behavior* (1942), *Phenomenology of Perception* (1945), *Humanism and Terror* (1947), and *Sense and Non-Sense* (1948).[6] Hubert Damisch, in his introduction to the 1964 *Bulletin de psychologie* collection, indicates how much of a surprise this appointment was for those who already knew Merleau-Ponty's work: [7]

> University life has its detours and its crossroads, its paths of replacement (as Merleau-Ponty said of behavior), and its transversal phenomena. And certainly in the Autumn of 1949, some of us were astonished to see the philosopher of the *Phenomenology of Perception*, the polemicist of *Humanism and Terror*, the companion of Sartre on *Les Temps modernes,* called to the Sorbonne to teach Child Psychology and Pedagogy. With astonishment, a sense of disappointment undoubtedly arises also. In confusion we had awaited from the discipline of philosophy, as it is taught, an opening up of this language, this new speech which we had known up to that point only in writing and which remained voiceless for us. We had expected it to come from philosophy, but not initially from psychology and even less from child psychology or pedagogy. . . .

In actual fact, Merleau-Ponty was not just a name on a book; he was not entirely unknown to French students. In 1947–48, Merleau-Ponty gave a course at the Ecole Normale Superieure entitled: *L'Union de l'âme et du corps chez Malbranche, Biran et Bergson* (*The Union of Body and Soul according to Malbranche, Biran, and Bergson*).[8] In 1948–49, he lectured there on *Saussure.*[9] Philosophy students at the University of Lyon had also had the opportunity to hear Merleau-Ponty from 1945–46 to 1947–48. Tilliette lists the following course titles: *La Liberté chez Leibnitz*

6. Maurice Merleau-Ponty, *Humanism and Terror,* trans. John O'Neill (Boston: Beacon Press, 1969); *Sense and Non-Sense,* trans. Hubert L. and Patricia A. Dreyfus (Evanston, Ill.: Northwestern University Press, 1964).

7. Hubert Damisch currently teaches at the Ecole Pratique des Hautes Etudes, Section VI.

8. Published as *L'Union de l'âme et du corps chez Malbranche, Biran et Bergson,* ed. Jean Deprun (Paris: Vrin, 1968).

9. These lectures are unpublished.

(*Freedom according to Leibnitz*) in 1946–47; *Âme et corps chez Malbranche, Maine de Biran et Bergson* (*Body and Soul according to Malbranche, Maine de Biran, and Bergson*) in 1947–48; and *Langage et Communication* (*Language and Communication*) in 1947–48.[10] He offered the second of the three concurrently at Lyon and at the Ecole Normale in Paris.

Somewhat conflicting titles and course matter have been suggested by Fernand Jacquet, who has kindly allowed me to see the lecture notes that he took during Merleau-Ponty's lectures at the University of Lyon.[11] From these notes it appears that a 1945–46 course was devoted to psychological methods. Here Merleau-Ponty dealt principally with psychoanalysis, behaviorism, and Gestalt psychology. He then considered the history of theories concerning the nature of language. Some of the philosophers treated were: Heraclitus (language as a divine being, a magical force, and an expression of wisdom), Socrates (language as a reality in itself), Plato (the distinction between language and thought; language as expressing what consciousness envisions), Descartes (the possibility of a universal language and the notion that the creation of language presupposes an analysis of thought; an idea as that which consciousness envisions), Locke (language as playing a central role in the life of the mind; language as serving to support intellectual facts; language as a state of consciousness, as something to be experienced), Berkeley (the general word as not covering anything true; there are only particular experiences; language as giving an illusion of the universal; one must destroy this illusion and rediscover the consciousness that gives the individual and the concrete), Humboldt (language not as the production of the mind, but as mind realizing itself), Cassirer (language as a phenomenon of concrete expression with three relations: expression, presentation, signification). In this section, Merleau-Ponty was particularly interested in the relationship between language and thought, the role of consciousness in expression, and the significance of metaphor.

10. See the bibliography in Xavier Tilliette, *Merleau-Ponty* (Paris: Seghers, 1970).
11. Fernand Jacquet now teaches philosophy at a *lycée* in Paris.

Fernand Jacquet has notes for three courses in 1946–47, dealing with (1) genetic psychology; (2) aesthetics and modern painting; and (3) Durkheim and modern sociology. (1) The notes on genetic psychology again discuss Freudianism, behaviorism, and Gestalt theory, but also go into problems of causality, genesis, and play in the child; in short, they are presentations and commentaries on the major books which Piaget had published by that time (i.e. *The Child's Conception of the World, The Child's Conception of Physical Causality, Judgement and Reasoning in the Child, The Language and Thought of the Child, Play, Dreams and Imitation in Childhood,* and *The Child's Conception of Time*).[12] (2) The course on aesthetics ranges from a consideration of contemporary aesthetics, and a discussion of Cézanne, cinema, cubism, Malraux, to the significance of the psychology of art. Much of Merleau-Ponty's interest in this material is reflected in the first part of *Sense and Non-Sense*. (3) "Durkheim and Modern Sociology" is concerned principally with Merleau-Ponty's reflections on Emile Durkheim, J. S. Mill, and Max Weber.

The Jacquet notes for 1947–48 cover three more courses. (1) The first is on aesthetics, particularly modern poetry (focusing on the symbolists: Baudelaire, Rimbaud, and Mallarmé). At that time Merleau-Ponty tried to articulate the essence of poetry, with emphasis on Sartre's interpretation of Baudelaire and Valéry's study of Mallarmé.[13] (2) The second was a series of textual commentaries on the following books: Paul Guillaume's *La Psycho-*

---

12. Jean Piaget, *The Child's Conception of the World,* trans. Joan and Andrew Tomlinson (London: Routledge & Kegan Paul, 1929); *The Child's Conception of Physical Causality,* trans. Marjorie Gabain (London: Routledge & Kegan Paul, 1952); *Judgment and Reasoning in the Child,* trans. Marjorie Warden (London: Routledge & Kegan Paul, 1952); *The Language and Thought of the Child,* trans. Marjorie Gabain (Cleveland: Meridian, 1955); *Play, Dreams and Imitation in Childhood,* trans. C. Gattegno and F. M. Hodgson (New York: Norton, 1962); *The Child's Conception of Time,* trans. A. J. Pomerans (New York: Ballantine, 1969).

13. Jean-Paul Sartre, *Baudelaire* (Paris: Gallimard, 1947). Paul Valéry, *The Collected Works of Paul Valéry,* trans. M. Cowley and J. R. Lawler, Vol. VIII (Princeton, N.J.: Princeton University Press, 1971).

logie de la forme, Freud's *Introductory Lectures on Psychoanalysis,* and Lagache's *La Jalousie.*[14] (3) The third course was on psychology, but was devoted explicitly to language. This is the most important forerunner of *Consciousness and the Acquisition of Language.* It is probably also the same course that Tilliette has designated as "Language and Communication." Here Merleau-Ponty was concerned with three basic issues: (*a*) the critique of scientism, which manifests itself in psychology, linguistics, sociology, and history; (*b*) the relationship between language and thought; and (*c*) the speaking subject and his role in communication.

Significant portions of this material shed light upon the course translated here. However, extensive commentary would be required in order to specify the differences and similarities between these two stages in Merleau-Ponty's reflections on language.[15] The present work represents the final and most mature development of these courses on language.

In translating *Consciousness and the Acquisition of Language,* I have included a table of contents and added a series of footnotes to the few that are found in the French text. Many of Merleau-Ponty's footnotes in the translation were originally incorporated within the text itself. Some subheads have also been added for the sake of symmetry and facility of reading. I have provided bibliographical information for those writers whom Merleau-Ponty mentions. English translations have been given, where available. In cases where only the name of a particular writer appears in the French text, I have wherever possible given in the footnotes the title of the book clearly under consideration. I have also taken the liberty to provide supplementary passages and comments where they might be useful.

---

14. Paul Guillaume, *La Psychologie de la forme* (Paris: Flammarion, 1937). Sigmund Freud, *Introductory Lectures on Psychoanalysis* (London: Allen & Unwin, 1922). Daniel Lagache, *La Jalousie amoureuse: Psychologie descriptive de psychoanalyse* (Paris: Presses Universitaires de France, 1947).

15. Many of the comments which occur in the earlier course (*Langage et communication*) were eventually incorporated into "The Metaphysical in Man," in *Sense and Non-Sense,* pp. 83–98.

The word *sens* has been translated as "meaning," while *signification* appears as "signification." Sometimes translators have given both terms as "meaning." I have kept them separate for the use of the reader who is at all concerned with the distinction. On the other hand, I have rendered *conduite* and *comportement* as "behavior" (although sometimes I translate *conduite* as "form of behavior"). Similarly, the distinction between *langue* and *langage,* which is not expressed in English, does not show up in the translation. Both French words are rendered as "language." *Ensemble* and *totalité* are two other terms that Merleau-Ponty uses quite often. *Totalité* always appears as "totality," but *ensemble* is given as either "whole" or "totality," according to the context. The term *autrui,* which occurs profusely in Merleau-Ponty, as it does in Sartre, means "other people" or "others," but it is a collective term used as a singular in French. At times, therefore, the ensuing context has required that it be translated as "another person" or "the other." This is perhaps an important distinction for the whole problem of intersubjectivity. Also, the terms *moi* and *soi* do not have exact equivalents in English. I have always rendered *moi* as "ego," "me," or "self," and *soi* as "self."

I am very grateful to my wife Terri for reading over the translation with me in its final stages. Her continued encouragement and understanding, along with her own knowledge of developmental psychology and language acquisition, were extremely helpful. Most of the translation was completed while I was in Paris during the 1971–72 academic year on a French Government Fellowship, with supplementary grants from the Alliance Française de New York and from the Center for Research in International Studies at Stanford University. I was also greatly assisted by Claude Lefort. He kindly helped place Northwestern University Press in contact with Madame Merleau-Ponty, who has graciously permitted this translation. Finally, I wish to thank Professor James M. Edie, who, in addition to providing an excellent introduction, first suggested that this translation be undertaken.

Consciousness and the
Acquisition of Language

Introduction

A. *The Reflexive Approach*

THE PROBLEM OF LANGUAGE is a problem for both philosophy and psychology. According to the philosophical tradition of Descartes and Kant, language is denied all philosophical meaning and becomes an exclusively technical problem.

In this Cartesian tradition, there is no plane on which consciousness and language meet. If one recognizes that consciousness is a unique type of being, then one will reject language as something outside consciousness and find that it is analogous to things. The interior link between consciousness and language no longer exists, for consciousness, to be conscious *of something,* must be consciousness of itself.[1] According to this view, consciousness is an activity of universal synthesis. Other people are nothing but the projection of what one knows of oneself. The implication of this philosophical principle is that one does not encounter others. This position escapes solipsism only by rejecting the requirement that consciousness be unique. Since we are

---

1. [My italics. All translator's notes will be enclosed in brackets, to distinguish them from Merleau-Ponty's footnotes.]

individual beings, we are isolated, but through thought we lift ourselves up to the level of the universal.

From this perspective, language arises from the order of things and not from the order of the subject. Spoken or written, words are physical phenomena that give rise to an accidental, fortuitous, and conventional link between the sense of the word and its physical aspect. Communication of consciousness is not possible; my words simply give other people a chance to remember what they already know. Language is an uttered message, but it does not itself imply effective communication. The word does not have any power of its own. Thus the best language would be the most neutral, and the best of all would be a scientific language, that is, the algorithm, where there is no possibility of equivocation. This preference is exemplified by the various attempts at constructing a universal language, for which a dictionary of human thought encompassing all languages and all thoughts would be needed.

From this perspective, one ends up by devaluating language. One considers it only as a piece of clothing for consciousness, an accouterment of thought. Even for a writer like Sartre, who does not ignore the problem of other people, it is impossible for language to present something to thought. The word has no "power"; it universalizes and summarizes what already exists. Here, thought owes nothing to the word.

B. *A New Approach to the Problem*

This Cartesian philosophy is an ally of the most positivist of sciences; it gives psychology complete license to treat language as an object. Take, for example, the now obsolete conception of aphasia as the loss of verbal images.

1. [*The signifying power of language.*] The agreement of a reflexive philosophy and of a mechanistic psychology is, however, dissolved on all sides by an evolution that identifies the problem. Sartre says that language provides no special difficulties of its own, but notes that, in its formulation, language does show the origin of new forms of behavior. Consider the example in Stendhal's *The Charterhouse of Parma,* when the Count fears the first

word of love that will confirm the young couple's feelings, which as yet have not been verbally expressed.

In general, one can no longer continue to base relations with others on the value of truth; one can no longer avoid recognizing others. The consequence of this recognition, as far as language is concerned, is that language must produce communication between individuals. Thus language becomes something mysterious, since it is neither a self nor a thing. Psychology has detected that a word is not a thing. This is why aphasia is no longer considered to be the loss of verbal images. The aphasic still knows how to put words together. He does not know how to say "red," but he can say "cherry-red." K. Goldstein says that aphasia is not the loss of a word, nor the loss of an idea, but it is the loss of "that which renders the word appropriate for expression." [2] Goldstein's view is that one must distinguish a meaningful [*plein de son sens*] word from one which is meaningless [*vidé de son sens*]—one must recognize the presence of meaning in the word.[3] This analysis shows us that language has a kind of signifying power.

2. *Influences from the evolution of linguistics.* According to Saussure, language is not a multiplicity of words or ideas in the service of whoever is speaking.[4] It is not a set of signs corresponding to a set of ideas, but rather it is a unique whole, in which each word gathers its signification through the others as a mass that is progressively differentiating itself.

For the linguist G. Guillaume, a sublinguistic scheme extends beneath each language, which informs us, for example, about the temporal architectonic in a given language.[5] However, this scheme is not *thought* by individuals. It is neither interior to the

2. [See, for example, Kurt Goldstein, *Language and Language Disturbances* (New York: Grune & Stratton, 1948). Other references to Goldstein's work on aphasia can be found in the bibliography to Merleau-Ponty's *Phenomenology of Perception,* trans. Colin Smith (London: Routledge & Kegan Paul, 1962).]

3. [Merleau-Ponty gives the German *sinnvoll* and *sinnlos*, but the English "meaningful" and "meaningless" perform the same function.]

4. [See Ferdinand de Saussure, *Course in General Linguistics,* trans. Wade Baskin (New York: McGraw-Hill, 1966).]

5. [See Gustave Guillaume's articles from 1933 to 1958, collected under the title: *Langage et science du langage* (Paris: Nizet, 1964).]

consciousness of the subject, nor an external reality. Therefore, since language is neither a thing nor a mind, we can postulate that it is characteristically obscure and ambiguous.

3. *Influences from literary experience.* The literary experience of language confirms these characteristics. In the last hundred years, language has been something other than a "clothing of thought" for writers. The classical writer had an absolute confidence in words. La Bruyère, for example, said that a good expression exists always, even if the writer has not found it.[6] After all, the classical writer postulated that language is already in things. J. Paulhan has analyzed this illusion by claiming that at the moment the thing is stated, it is as if it had always been stated.[7] The word actualizes the idea and allows itself to be forgotten: successful language and successful thought are one. Language is obscure in terms of its function, which is to render everything else clear. It cannot be observed or grasped directly; it can only be exercised.

C. *Conclusion*

Language is neither thing nor mind, but it is immanent and transcendent at the same time. However, we still have to discover

6. [See Jean de la Bruyère, *Les Caractères* (Paris: Larousse, 1954). In §1: On the Works of the Mind, no. 17, La Bruyère says, "Of all the different expressions which can render one of our thoughts, there is only one that is the right one. We do not always encounter it in speaking or in writing: it is nevertheless true that it exists, that any other expression is weaker and will not satisfy a man of intellect who wants to be understood" (my translation).]

7. [See Jean Paulhan, *Jacob Cow le pirate, ou Si les mots sont des signes* (1919–21), in *Oeuvres complètes* (Paris: Cercle du Livre Précieux, 1966), II, 128). Note, for example, the passage:

. . . it becomes a delicate question to explain that an idea sometimes follows a word, comes out of it, translates it. Cilia, who tries to explain to her doctor the nature of her daughter's illness, discovers, in speaking, the very thing that she feared, and is, herself, astonished by it. When Atys brings himself to say to Chrysus: "So you lied," each reconstructs his real thoughts from the words that were spoken. An idea here is a sign for the word, and, by comparison, we are far from having the word as a sign for the idea. Still, for a poet, we know that he is thrown in the midst of words, he urges them on, he listens to them, he awaits them (my translation).]

the laws that pertain to it. This problem will always be central to the study of language acquisition. The psychological examination of language will lead us to its clarifying function, and the psychological problem will lead us to the philosophical problem.

[II] [METHODOLOGY]

A. [*The Reflexive Method*]

As WE HAVE SEEN, language is invincible to all efforts that seek to convert it into an object. But evidence also indicates that it is not to be confused with mind. It does not satisfy the distinction between sign [*signe*] and signified [*signifié*]. We have seen that the reflexive method is powerless to study language. Will the inductive method be any more successful?

B. *The Inductive Method*

Let us begin by clarifying the notion of induction. John Stuart Mill held that induction is the simple process of recording natural correlations.[8] In his *Expérience humaine et la causalité physique*, Brunschvicg analyzed and opposed Mill's theory.[9] However, his position remains equivocal because of a contradiction between the two parts of his analysis. In the first part, he contested Mill's empirical attitude, for he claimed that the problem is not to indicate correlations between facts, but rather to define the variables between which the causal connection will be established. Hence, the first task is to actively make a hypothesis, and this is an intellectual task, since facts cannot be found in nature.

In the second part of his analysis, when Brunschvicg examined the relationships between hypotheses and existing facts, he concluded that the only verifiable element in induction is the

8. [See John Stuart Mill, *A System of Logic*, 2 vols. (London, 1843; 8th ed. 1872).]

9. [Léon Brunschvicg, *L'Expérience humaine et la causalité physique* (Paris: Alcan, 1922). Note particularly pt. I, bk. 3, on "External Experience."]

sum of the numerical relations existing between the different variables of the phenomenon. That which is verified is not the image of the facts which the hypothesis gives us, but only the sum of the equations established between the facts. Even if the theory (the image of the facts) is refuted by that which follows, the equations retain some meaning as long as they are translated into the language of the new hypothesis.

Thus, on the one hand, Brunschvicg shows that induction is not a collection of given facts. It is an intellectual project. But, on the other hand, since induction represents the essence of the phenomena that are under investigation, its conclusions cannot be verified.

Can one, then, hope to understand the structure of language from the inductive method? We do not think that the relations between variables can elucidate the nature of language for us, and that is all that induction can do.

C. *The Phenomenological Method*

Neither of the two preceding methods can help us. However, there is a third possibility, which involves coming into contact with the facts, understanding them in themselves, reading them, and interpreting them so as to give them a meaning. We will have to vary the phenomenon in order to disclose a common signification from these variations. And the criterion for this method will not be a multiplicity of facts which will serve as proofs for pre-defined hypotheses. The proof will be in our fidelity to the phenomena, that is, in the precise hold [*la prise étroite*] which we will have of the materials used and, to some extent, in our "proximity" to pure description.

Consider the following use of this method in recent animal psychology: observers of animal behavior, after having used a method which continually projected human consciousness into the observed phenomena, were subsequently obliged to take on a strictly objective attitude. But soon this attitude showed itself to be insufficient. Thus, Koehler, in his rigorous experiments on the intelligence of apes, uses a particular method in which he is not content simply to calculate that which is measurable.[10] He finds that attending exclusively to the measurable is insufficient for a description of the phenomenon in its entirety. In describing the behavior of apes, he uses terms which could be taken as "anthropomorphic," like "found the solution by chance" or "by a fortunate mistake," that is, terms which are qualitatively distinctive. Since the objective (quantitative) result is the same, whether the ape finds a solution through comprehension or by chance, one cannot be restricted entirely to the purely quantitative analysis. By saying that "the ape solved the problem," Koehler introduces a kind of anthropomorphism, but one which is indispensable. He claims that we must go beyond quantitative analysis because there are truly noticeable differences in the behavior (namely, arriving at an exact solution is a melodic and continuous movement, whereas the solution found by chance is abrupt and discontinuous). We must, therefore, be subjective, since there is subjectivity in the situation—but that is not to say that we must be arbitrary.

Does Koehler proceed by induction? Yes, in the sense that although there is a hypothesis he appeals to facts that a hypothesis cannot explain. But, if he enters into the analysis of the intrinsic characteristics [*caractères*] of the phenomenon, it is so that the life of the animal will not be reduced to the behavior which is under observation. We cannot make what the observed animal offers us into an abstraction—we cannot separate out our human attitudes.

Others, like Koffka, clearly indicate the nature of the "descriptive concepts" which are the basis of this method and which, in psychology, are now beginning to clarify "functional characteristics." [11] Koffka and Koehler say that this appeal to our experience of observed behavior is "phenomenological." This method is new in that effective knowledge is not only measurable but also

10. [See Wolfgang Koehler, *The Mentality of Apes*, trans. Ella Winter (London: Routledge & Kegan Paul, 1925).]

11. [See, for example, Kurt Koffka, *The Growth of the Mind*, trans. Robert Morris Ogden (New York: Harcourt, Brace & Co. 1927), and particularly chap. 1: Problem and Method.]

qualitatively descriptive. This qualitative knowledge is not subjective; it is intersubjective. It describes that which is observable by all.

This is the method that we will adopt for the study of language. We will study facts, not in order to verify some hypothesis that transcends them, but to give an internal meaning [*un sens intérieur*] to the facts themselves. Of utmost importance will be the rigor with which one embraces the totality as well as the details of certain facts.

This is the method that Goldstein admirably utilizes in his study of aphasia and agnosia. Instead of considering the same symptom in many subjects, he addresses himself to the complete analysis of one single subject, striving to explore all areas of behavior. This is a method of understanding which is no less rigorous than the other, for, where induction seeks out a multiplicity of facts, Goldstein's method explores in depth and cuts into the core of one single case.

In conclusion, we propose to apply a method that Bergson had defined but hardly ever practiced: he held that philosophy must uncover the meaning of those phenomena which are described by scientists. The role of philosophy is to reconstitute the world just as the physicist sees it, but with the "fringe" which the physicist does not mention and which is furnished by his contact with the qualitative world.[12] This program remains valid, since for us there is no difference between psychology and philosophy. Psychology is always an implicit and budding philosophy, and philosophy has never given up its contact with facts.

On this basis, in order to understand the being of language, we will address ourselves to the following points:

(1) the psychological development of the child;

(2) the facts concerning the disintegration of language;

(3) the approach of linguistics to language;

(4) the experience which literature represents. (To become a writer is to learn a personal language. The writer creates his own language and his own public. He, therefore, recommences the creation of language on a higher level.)

12. See Henri Bergson, *Introduction to Metaphysics,* trans. T. E. Hulme (Indianapolis: Bobbs-Merrill, 1913).

1 / The Psychological Development of Language in the Child

[I] An Overview

DURING THE FIRST MONTHS OF LIFE, the child cries; he makes expressive movements; and then he begins to babble. One must consider this babbling as the ancestor of language: it is, above all, extraordinarily rich and includes phonemes which do not exist in the language that is spoken around the child, and which he himself, once he has become an adult, is incapable of reproducing (for example, when he wants to reacquire them to learn a foreign language). This babbling is therefore a polymorphic language, which is spontaneous with respect to its environment. (It exists in deaf-mute children, even though it is not as well developed.) There is, however, a large amount of imitation. This imitation reaches its culmination between six and twelve months, but it remains rudimentary to the extent that the child does not grasp the meaning of that which he is imitating. The same relationship exists between babbling and language as between scribbling and drawing.

This imitation concerns the melody of the sentence just as much as the words, because the child tries, as it were, to speak "in general." W. Stern relates that, for a month, his daughter spoke a foreign "language," which had a conversational tone but which did not mean anything.[1] (It was as though she were playing

1. [See William Stern, *Psychology of Early Childhood* (New York: Holt, 1931).]

at speaking.) According to Delacroix, "The child bathes in language."[2] He is attracted and enthralled by the movement of dialogue around him, and tries it himself.

Language is the indissoluble extension of all physical activity, and at the same time it is quite new in relation to that physical activity. Speech emerges from the "total language" as constituted by gestures, mimicries, etc. . . . But speech transforms. Already it uses the organs of phonation for a function that is unnatural to them—in effect, language has no organs. All the organs that contribute to language already have another function (Sapir).[3] Language introduces itself as a superstructure, that is, as a phenomenon that is already a witness to another order.

The problem is to know how it has passed from a quasibiological activity to one which is nonbiological, but which nevertheless presupposes a whole movement, or activity, that has integrated it into dialogue.

In the ensuing period, from nine to eighteen months—fifteen months on the average—spoken language begins. First the child knows how to say a few words; then there is a kind of stagnation: Preyer's son continued for six months with only two words, and Stern's son for two months with one single word.[4] In a less precise fashion, this phenomenon occurs in most children, for language has a kind of incubation period.

[II] THE ACQUISITION OF LANGUAGE DURING THE FIRST YEAR

A. *The First Weeks*

A YOUNG CHILD'S FACIAL EXPRESSIONS are quite precocious. Grégoire indicates that the nursing infant, up to the end

2. [See Henri Delacroix, *Le Langage et la pensée* (Paris: Alcan, 1924).]

3. [See Edward Sapir, *Language* (New York: Harcourt, Brace & World, 1921).]

4. [See Thierry Wilhelm Preyer, *The Mind of the Child*, trans. H. W. Brown (New York: Appleton, 1914).]

of the second month, laughs and smiles, not only to demonstrate its satisfaction, but also to answer to the smile of those around him.[5] This already presumes a relationship with others, which precedes the language that will appear in this context.

This is why it is artificial to consider the first words as spontaneous. Long before they appeared, there had been attitudinal responses. Grégoire emphasizes the fact that the intellectual activity of the nursing infant is much more important than we would think. We have a tendency to underestimate it, since it is not accompanied by any external manifestations. Yet, from birth, there is a capacity for relating to the external world that does not stop growing during the first weeks of life. One can even stimulate conditioned reflexes in the embryo, and, from the moment of birth, the brain records specific changes occurring in the immediate environment.

The ability to mimic is considerably enhanced during the first week, as is hearing and vision: a child from four to seven days old hears one and a half times better than a child from zero to three days old. Premature children have a normal intellectual development, for they are able to overcome the physical handicap that they had at birth.

B. *Babbling*

1. [*Two and a half months.*] From two and a half months on, babbling appears. It is formed principally with the consonants [*l*] and [*r*], whose acquisition cannot be explained in terms of imitation. These vocal utterances seem to be common to all babies, independent of the language around them. One could explain the use of these phenomena from a physiological point of view by showing that the predominance of sucking activity favors the appearance of labial and gutteral consonants.

It seems untenable to claim that the babbling of the first period is a result of imitation. Some writers believe that it has to do with an imitation of lip movement. But P. Guillaume has

5. [Antoine Grégoire, *L'Apprentissage du langage*, Vol. I (Gembloux: Duculot, 1937).]

shown that children imitate gutterals which cannot be seen [*invisible*] on the lips of the person speaking.[6] If there is any influence from the environment, it is hearing and not vision that evokes the imitation. Moreover, children fix not upon the mouth but rather on the eyes of the person speaking. It has often been noted that children open their mouths when they are listening to someone speak; but Grégoire claims that this has to do with the contagiousness of the other person's behavior (like yawning), and not with an effort to reconstruct that which has been seen.

But the presence of the adult's language stimulates [*excite*] the child in a general way: from his first waking moments, the child hears someone speaking. Most of the time, language is addressed to him directly, and this acoustic sensation provokes the stimulation, first, of his limbs, and then, of the phonatory organs (assimilable by the limbs).

In conclusion, the child receives the "sense" of language from his environment. Imitation plays absolutely no part at this stage. However, one must emphasize the importance of the child's involvement in the mode of speech of his environment (i.e., rhythm, pitch, etc.), the effect of which is a general attraction to language. (Again, remember Delacroix's statement: "The child bathes in language.") Wundt says that the development of language is always a "premature" development.[7] In fact, it is impossible to deny a kind of spontaneity; but the child's relationship with his environment is what points him toward language. It is a development toward an end defined by the environment and not preestablished in the organism.

2. *Four months.* From four to ten months, according to Grégoire, an important linguistic and intellectual development takes place. However, we are less aware of it because we are much more attuned to the progress of motor activity. What is the significance of sounds uttered during this period? The child lingers at certain sounds and modulates them, varying their ac-

6. [See Paul Guillaume, *Imitation in Children*, trans. Elaine P. Halperin (Chicago: University of Chicago Press, 1971).]

7. [See Wilhelm Wundt's major work, *Principles of Physiological Psychology*, trans. E. B. Titchener (London: Sonnenschein, 1904).]

cent and duration, all of which can be translated into variations of energy and disposition [*humeur*]. From this moment on, certain appreciable nuances, drawn from the speech of adults, begin to appear. Bühler, in his "theory of language," has observed that German children initially place the tonic accent on the second syllable of their vocal utterances, but quickly shift it to the first syllable.[8] They take on, as it were, "the German accent." Thus, even before speaking, the child appropriates the rhythm and stress [*accentuation*] of his own language.

About this time, children achieve vocal utterances of an extraordinary richness, emitting sounds that they will be incapable of reproducing later. There will be a selection, a kind of impoverishment.

3. *Seven months.* Around the seventh month, the free babbling seems to be transformed little by little into a voluntary effort to speak. The child is still far from articulated speech, but he does make some attempts at pronunciation, and he becomes more and more sensitive to what he hears. It is as if his intention to speak has become more and more definite.

4. *Eight months.* In the eighth month, the child can begin to repeat words when they are spoken to him with the expectation that he will repeat them. He introduces these words into a kind of sentence, that is, a kind of imitation of the sentence according to its rhythmic aspect. This is the pseudo-language.

5. *Twelve months.* From the tenth to the twelfth month, Grégoire noticed a polyphony of pseudo-words with an infinite number of variations. Also, around twelve months, his son amused himself by crying out louder than his father. In this way he became capable of creating quasi-linguistic effects.

C. *The First Word*

It is at this moment, writes Grégoire, that his son's first word appeared, a word designating the train which passed in front of

8. [See Karl Bühler, *Sprachtheorie: Die Darstellungsfunktion der Sprache* (Jena: Fischer, 1934).]

his house. This was a particular word which gave a name to a single thing, or set of things (the train, the emotion released by its passing, etc.). Above all, it translated an affective state. The multiplicity of meanings [*pluralité de sens*] was contained in the word-sentence.[9]

It would be artificial to draw an absolute division between the first word and that which was there before. For a long time, the child had defined objects (by his behavior); he simply did not make use of particular words. In the Grégoire case, we cannot say that the appearance of the first word implies a sudden consciousness [*prise de conscience*] of the sign-signified relationship.

In a *Journal de psychologie* article, Cassirer said that the first word allows for a synthesis of impressions and disparate facts.[10] This presupposes that the word arrives as a summing up and a pruning down of a larger, unformulated richness of experience. For Grégoire, on the contrary, the experience prior to the word is poorer and less complete. For him, the word emerges as a unity. It is not a synthesis of prior experiences.

Grégoire has attempted to show the continuity of language development. On the one hand, there is the expression and definition of the object, even before the appearance of the first word. On the other hand, this appearance does not in any way put an end to the babbling, which, for a long time, accompanies the child's speech [*parole*]. And perhaps certain aspects of the adult's interior language, which is often not formulated, are no more than a continuation of the babbling. On the one hand, from the beginning of life, there are anticipations of what will become language. On the other hand, there is a persistence, right up into adulthood, of what was previously babbling.

9. [In current psycholinguistic terminology this phenomenon is called "holophrastic speech." See David McNeill, *The Acquisition of Language* (New York: Harper & Row, 1970), p. 20.]

10. [See Ernst Cassirer, "Le Langage et la construction du monde des objets," *Journal de psychologie normale et pathologique*, XXX (Jan.–April, 1933) 18–44. This whole issue has been republished as *Essais sur le langage*, presented by Jean-Claude Pariente (Paris: Editions de minuit, 1969). The Cassirer article appears on pp. 37–68.]

D. *Meaning* [11] *of the First Word*

1. *The intellectualist interpretation.* One is tempted to say with Delacroix that the sign is not really a "signifier" [*signifiant*] unless it is a "mental sign." [12] For that reason, it is necessary that connections be established between words, and that a logical principle, a formal relation, regulate their relationships. The sign therefore will be part of the context, and its signification will depend on the context in which it is implicated.

Delacroix and W. Stern seem to be in agreement on the importance of the first word. [13] It reveals to the child that each thing has a name, and it accounts for his desire to learn these names. They hold that the appearance of the first words suddenly makes *the relationship of the sign to the signified* explicit.

This conception bears largely on the famous example of Helen Keller, the deaf-mute blind girl, whose teacher succeeded in reeducating her through the sense of touch. [14] She relates in her autobiography that for a long time all efforts to give her a notion of the sign were in vain. But one day, when she was scooping up some water, at the moment that the contact of the cold water on her hand keenly impressed her, her teacher traced on her other hand the conventional sign designating water. At this instant, Helen Keller suddenly understood the sign-signified relationship, and, within an hour, she had learned about thirteen new signs.

This example has encouraged the "all or nothing" view: either one has consciousness and comprehension, or one has no language at all.

2. *Critique of this view.* Does the appearance of the first word signify the sudden consciousness [*prise de conscience*] of the

11. [Merleau-Ponty uses the word *signification* here.]

12. Henri Delacroix, *Le Langage et la pensée* (Paris: Alcan, 1924).

13. William Stern, *Psychology of Early Childhood* (New York: Holt, 1931).

14. [See Helen Keller, *The Story of My Life* (New York, 1903), p. 316.]

sign-signified relationship? There are several reasons why this seems to be difficult to accept.

(a) If this were the case, the child's first word would be followed by a rapid progress, as in Helen Keller's example. In fact, most of the time, it is followed by a long stagnation. How can we explain this stagnation if the first word really results in a sudden consciousness of the sign?

(b) Stern himself has admitted that the child is far from possessing a concept of the sign in the way that an adult understands it. For the adult, the sign is a convention. For the child, up to six or seven years old, it is a property, a quality of the thing.[15] For the child, the sign has a quasi-magical relationship, a relationship of participation, an intimate resemblance with the signified [signifié]. Stern himself has related the example of a young child's creation of words. This child, when questioned much later as to the reason for his creations, said matter-of-factly: "because the thing seemed to have that name." [16]

(c) The child's first words are often distinct from adult words. Often they are uttered according to their onomatopoetic value (hence the relationship through resemblance). But even if the child uses an adult word, the meaning is always more ephemeral. Often a single word will designate a group of things are applicable to a similar situation (for example, "music" for: music, military music, and soldiers).

Neither in this case, nor when he seems to be using a metaphor, does the child make any generalizations; he lacks concepts for that. The child possesses a syncretic view of the situation, which allows him to assimilate things in a different order.

Hence, if the word has such a slippery and confusing meaning for the child, we can no longer presume that he knows the sign in the same way that we do (in this case, its representation would be more coherent from the outset). However, the acquisi-

---

15. Note the observations of Jean Piaget, particularly in *The Construction of Reality in the Child*, trans. Margaret Cook (New York: Basic Books, 1954).

16. [. . . *parce que la chose avait l'air de s'appeler comme cela*. The French implies that the thing has actively and reflexively called itself by the word which the child has uttered.]

tion of the first word does mark a decisive step in the acquisition of language. In what way can we understand this phenomenon?

[III] THE ACQUISITION OF LANGUAGE IN THE FIRST FIVE YEARS

A. *Eighteen Months to Three Years*

DURING THIS PERIOD, the child directs his attention primarily toward a more and more perfect acquisition of his maternal tongue. The role of imitation predominates at this time, but it pertains only to the piecemeal textual production of the language spoken around him. One must distinguish between immediate imitation and deferred imitation (where the model is incorporated into the child's latent knowledge and is not used until later). One famous example of deferred imitation is that of Stumpf's son. After having acquired several words and many natural symbols (onomatopoeia, interjection, etc.), he went on for two years without any increase in his vocabulary, manifesting a kind of passive resistance, a bad faith with respect to language, in spite of his nearly complete comprehension.

At about three years and three months, he suddenly abandoned this attitude and immediately began speaking with ease. In this case, as in other less clear-cut situations, we are talking about a true organization of imitated models and never of pure and simple reception and reproduction. (We will examine this problem of imitation further.)

B. *After Three Years*

Can we distinguish other stages that follow? This seems difficult to do. Stern has distinguished the passing from word to sentence. However, this is not a very well-defined stage, since the first words always have a sentence value, even though the strict distinction is debatable.

Other people distinguish different stages according to the growth of vocabulary and take stock of the child's linguistic knowledge at different ages. There have been a number of studies of this nature with disconcerting and always disappointing results. Mme Descoeudres evaluated the vocabulary of children at about three and a half years and on this basis established tests to avoid the necessity of repeating the evaluation each time.[17] The results are varied. (Stern found 300 words at two years; Deville, 688; Major, 142.) What is the reason for this diversity of results?

1. There is a lack of an exact definition of what must count as *a* word. (Do two suffixes for one root count as two words, or one word? The same for flectional endings, etc.)

2. The working vocabulary of an adult, as well as a child, is much more limited than the vocabulary he understands or which he would know how to use if he really felt the necessity. (Vendryes has said that this virtual vocabulary is impossible to inventory.) [18] One cannot consider linguistic equipment as a summation of words. Rather, we must appeal to systems of variation that render an open series of words possible. This cannot be explored further here. It is a totality of open sectors with infinite possibilities of expression. Thus, when a child appropriates a new meaning for a word that he knows, must we count this as a new word? Yes and no, for we see that a word is truly a whole and not a summation.

C. *Five Years*

Perhaps, as Piaget has suggested, one could introduce a new level of development after the age of five. Up to that point the child does not seek to communicate with others (dialogue) as much as to talk by himself (monologue). Speech, as a mode of social communication, does not gain importance until the child is seven or eight years old.

In his experiments with kindergarten children at the Institut Jean-Jacques Rousseau, Piaget has come up with a ratio of 46 percent nonsocialized talk (juxtaposed monologue). But Mrs. Müchow, in a Hamburg kindergarten, found only 30 percent.

17. See Alice Descoeudres, *Le Developpement de l'enfant de deux à sept ans* (Neuchâtel: Delachaux & Niestlé, n. d.), particularly chap. 5, where the results are reported.]

18. [See Joseph Vendryes, *Language: A Linguistic Introduction to History*, trans. Paul Radin (New York: Barnes & Noble, 1951).]

This could be due to a difference in the system of education: the children in Piaget's center had been raised according to the Montessori method, while those in Hamburg were largely accustomed to a life in groups.

David Katz, in his observations, has counted 150 quasi-familiar conversations of his children (five years, and three and a half years), and he has detected true discussions, indications of curiosity, of feelings, etc., in their conversations with adults. He has noticed an actual [*réelle*] activation of speech, going far beyond Piaget's conception of egocentric language.[19]

Therefore, one must be wary of all artificial divisions into "successive stages." It appears that, from the beginning, all the possibilities are inscribed in the expressive manifestations of the child. There is never anything absolutely new, but there are anticipations, regressions, and retentions of older elements in new forms. This development, where, on the one hand, everything is sketched out in advance, and which, on the other hand, proceeds according to a discontinuously progressive series, denies intellectualist as well as empiricist theories.[20] The Gestaltists have helped us to understand the problem better by explaining how, at decisive periods of development, the child appropriates linguistic *Gestalten*, general structures, neither by an intellectual effort nor by an immediate imitation. To elucidate this problem we will consider in turn: (1) the problem of the acquisition of phonemes; and (2) the problem of imitation.

[IV] [THE APPROPRIATION OF LINGUISTIC STRUCTURES]

A. *The Acquisition of Phonemes*

1. [*Presentation of Jakobson's position.*] When one poses the problem of language acquisition at the level of the *word,* one

---

19. [David Katz, *Conversations with Children* (London: Kegan, Paul, Trench, Trubner & Co., 1936).]

20. [Merleau-Ponty elucidates at length the nature of the empiricist and intellectualist positions in chaps. 1–3 of the "Introduction" to his *Phenomenology of Perception,* trans. Colin Smith (London: Routledge & Kegan Paul, 1962), pp. 3–51.]

encounters a major difficulty: the word refers to a certain concept, which already contains a duality, i.e., the formal distinction between sign and signified.

However, it is possible to approach language on the *phonemic* level. Phonemes do not make reference to any meaning at all; they are elements of language, which by themselves are deprived of meaning, but which do differentiate one word from another. That they have no signification by themselves does not signify that they are insignificant. Reflection on the phoneme allows one to surpass the distinction between sign and concept. Such a reflection allows one to determine the order (neither intellectual nor imitative) to which language acquisition belongs.

We follow Jakobson's analysis in which he proposes to compare the child's acquisition of a phoneme to the regression of the phonemic system in the case of aphasia.[21] Jakobson thinks that this system constitutes such a rigorous whole, with such strong lines of necessity, that its order of acquisition and disappearance is *invariable,* and never optional.[22]

Jakobson starts with the distinction between a specifying attitude [*esprit particulariste*] and a unifying attitude [*esprit unificateur*] (Saussure), both of which contribute to the formation of a language and to the maintenance of an equilibrium. Consider the case of children who, for a long time, refuse to speak the colloquial language [*langue ambiant*], as in the case of future poets (where this refusal can be the sign of a specific ability), women's language in certain tribes, and the language of lovers. The existence of a specifying attitude is undeniable, but it soon absorbs itself into a unifying attitude. Take, for example, the child who uses "baby" talk, but who revolts against the adult who condescends to speak to him in the same way.

How should we understand the systematic and regular order

21. Roman Jakobson, a study appearing in Sweden in 1941. [This is certainly the study entitled *Kindersprache, Aphasie und allgemeine Lautgesetze* (Uppsala: Almqvist & Wiksell, 1941). It has been translated by A. Keiler as *Child Language, Aphasia, and General Sound Laws* (The Hague: Mouton, 1968).]

22. There is no objection to be made against the comparison between a child and a sick person, since only the phonemic system, and not language as a totality, is in question.

of the appearance of phonemes? Physiologists would gladly invoke a "principle of minimum energy," but, in fact, there is no phoneme that is simpler or more difficult in itself. One must explain this order according to certain "privileged" behaviors constituting the constants of a given language. They are not easier in themselves. They do not lend themselves to being associated with some principle. They are the ultimate givens of the linguistic whole, allowing a maximum of efficiency to be realized.

Thus the phonemic system appears as an irreducible reality, and language acquisition appears as the integration of an individual into the structure of his language. This becomes very clear in the transition from babbling to the articulation of words. Here, there is what Jakobson calls a deflation: suddenly the richness of babbling disappears; the child loses not only the unused sounds in his language, but also many of those that would be very useful to him. Thus, the child who, in his babbling, differentiated perfectly his [k]s and [t]s, all of a sudden loses the possibility of differentiating them, although he recognizes them very well when an adult speaks them. It is, therefore, not a question of motor or auditory models posing a problem for him. Everything happens as though the child were obliged to restrain himself, because sounds now take on a distinctive signification. From the moment that phonemes serve to differentiate one word from another, the child manifests a need to appropriate their new value for himself, to gradually acquire their system of opposition and of original succession. In all, his capacity to pronounce depends not on his capacity to articulate (he had it at the stage of babbling), but on the acquisition of phonemic contrasts and their significative value. The rigorous order in which the child incorporates himself suggests to him the possibility of its linguistic value. Jakobson defines this phenomenon as: "the system of phonemic oppositions tending toward signification."

Where does Jakobson's notion concerning the "deflation" of vocal manifestations come from? The child ceases to be able to utter certain sounds as soon as he begins to speak, but this is due neither to some articulatory impossibility nor to the fact that he ceases to hear them. What happens is that he temporarily ceases to be able to pronounce them as *significative utterances* because they are not yet part of his significant phonemic system.

When the child, stimulated by the surrounding environment [*milieu ambiant*], wants to speak in turn, he sees a certain number of stable "structures" in language; he identifies them, and experiences their intersubjective value. He guesses the meaning [*sens*] that lies behind the reappearance of certain phonemes. He begins to employ them as "rules of usage" for his vocalization. This prepares him to give them a signification, but, at first, a confused situational signification.

The originality of Jakobson's theory consists in a narrow correlation between the adoption of a phonemic system in itself and its communicative function. On the whole, the structure of this system, as it is used, already invites signification. By dint of what he has heard spoken, the child guesses that signs are in question. The phonemic system draws signification as if through the interstices [*en creux*].

But Jakobson is less concerned with defining the ontological status of the phonemic system than with enumerating its properties: his study is more that of a scientist [*savant*] than of a philosopher.

He emphasizes the autonomy of this system: its structure is rigid; its rules refer only to the structure itself and not to psychological conditions exterior to it. At the point where language appears in the child, the rigidity of the system is masked by the persistence of babbling. The child continues to employ onomatopoeia and interjections which are not placed under the rules of the phonemic system (and which sometimes contribute to its enrichment).

For example, a child does not yet know how to pronounce an [r] in the context of language, but he uses it without any trouble when imitating bird songs. He knows how to pronounce it as long as he doesn't have to use it for speaking. This can be compared to the reeducation of stutterers. They are provided with situations in which they become accustomed to pronouncing the [r] by imitating the turning over of a motor, for example. After that, they are encouraged to integrate it into their language.

The author proposes to offer a counterproof for his theory by applying it to aphasiacs. Since the possession of language depends upon the integration of phonemes, inversely, aphasia must result in the destruction of the phonemic system. In the case of all pure aphasiacs, Jakobson establishes a regular disintegration of this system, often accompanied by a provisional reequilibration.[23] He has observed, for example, a Czech who lost the distinction between long and short vowels. Since the Czech language places the tonic accent on the first syllable, this patient compensated for his incapacity by placing the tonic accent on the penultimate syllable. Thus, he replaced the qualitative difference between vowels by a more energetic accentuation of words.

According to Jakobson, in aphasiacs, there subsists a system of phonemes, a unity, a degenerate [*dégradé*] whole that nevertheless remains systematic as a result of this continual reequilibration. One question arises from this situation: how is this work of equilibration experienced by the aphasiac?

An aphasiac can no longer pronounce certain words, even though he is neither agnosic, nor apraxic. His words are lost only insofar as they are part of a whole. Jakobson here uses Husserl's comparison to a game of chess. One can consider the chess pieces either according to their matter, or according to their signification in the game. Language is attained not as an articulatory phenomenon, but as an element of a linguistic game. In aphasia it is not the innate instrument that is lost, but the possibility of using it in certain cases.

It is only in the second part of his work that Jakobson attempts to define a phoneme. It is, he says: "*the element of language which, as far as this phoneme is concerned, distinguishes one word from all other words identical to it. They are*

23. [For an extensive discussion of equilibration and reequilibration, see *The Structure of Behavior*, trans. Alden L. Fischer (Boston: Beacon, 1963). Merleau-Ponty refers, for example, to the notion of form as a totality of forces in a state of equilibrium or of constant change such that no law is formulable for each part taken separately and such that each vector is determined in size and direction by all the others. Thus each local change in a form will be translated by a redistribution of forces which assures the constancy of their relation. It is this internal circulation which *is* the system as a physical reality (p. 137). On the vital level, "the internal determinants of this equilibrium are not given by a plurality of vectors, but by a general attitude toward the world" (p. 148).]

diacritic elements of language." As a consequence, phonemes are essential constituents of words, even though, in themselves, they are completely deprived of meaning. For example, the phoneme /i/ alone differentiates "pit" and "pat," but /i/ in itself does not mean anything.[24] These are, so to speak, signs of the first order: they relate not to things, as words do, but to words themselves.

However, since phonemes are the elements that differentiate words and since words relate to objects, disorders in the phonemic system often take on the same aspect as the disorders of language per se and often have the same result: homonymy. Jakobson takes as an example the two German words: *Rippe* ("ribs") and *Lippe* ("lips"). The only phoneme which differentiates *Rippe* from *Lippe* is the /r/. Two disorders are possible:

(*a*) The aphasiac cannot distinguish the /l/ from the /r/; he is obliged to use the same word for the two things.

(*b*) The aphasiac has lost the meaning of the words: for him, these are two distinct words, but he can no longer differentiate them, since they have no meaning for him—one of the two words falls outside of usage, the other serves for both cases. There is homonymy in the two cases, either by the destruction of the phonemic system or by the disappearance of the meaning of the words.

But, in all cases, disorders of the linguistic faculty are in question. They can be disorders of formation or of the symbolic function. Phonologists no longer restrict the notion of "symbolic function" to words. They integrate the whole phonemic system into it, since they claim that there is a close parallel between phonemes and words. Both are elements of the linguistic chain, and they differentiate the whole of which they are a part:

(*a*) The word, like the phoneme, has its own properties, its own constant forms.

(*b*) Both result in modifications with respect to their relationships (the phoneme modifies words, the word modifies the sentence).

(*c*) The two find their place in the whole because of their

24. [Merleau-Ponty cites the phoneme /an/ as it distinguishes *sang* from *saint* in French.]

properties in the series (laws of the phonemic system for the phoneme, laws of syntax for the word).

As for the phonemic system, it is composed, on the one hand, of a universal system common to all languages (in the child who is beginning to speak, it is the first thing that appears), and, on the other hand, of a particular system specific to each language which distinguishes one language from another. The child specifically determines this after he has acquired the elementary system.[25]

The order of phonemic succession is rigorous and invariable:

Palatals appear after dentals (/d/ is replaced by /k/).

The first vowel is /a/.

Then there are oppositions of consonants:

(a) /p/–/m/

(b) /p/–/t/

(c) /m/–/n/

This is the minimum consonantism according to which all child language begins.

Then the system of vowels develops:

(a) /a/–/i/ or /a/–/e/

(b) /u/ or /e/

This is the minimum vocalism.

Anterior consonants always appear before posterior consonants. There will be, therefore, in every language "founding" [*fondant*] elements and "founded" [*fondé*] elements.[26] The latter cannot appear before the former, which cannot disappear without resulting in the abolition of the "founded" elements.

25. According to Trubetzkoy, in the strictest sense, there is no universal composing element. [Nikolai Sergieevich Trubetzkoy, *Introduction to the Principles of Phonological Description*, trans. L. A. Murray (The Hague: Nijhoff, 1968).]

26. [Jakobson has also called the "founding" elements "primary units" and the "founded" elements "secondary units." The secondary units depend upon the existence of the primary units. See, for example, Roman Jakobson, "The Sound Laws of Child Language and their Place in General Phonology," in *Child Language: A Book of Readings*, ed. A. Bar-Adon and W. F. Leopold (Englewood Cliffs, N.J.: Prentice-Hall, 1971), pp. 75–82.]

This order of appearance is irreversible. In the case of aphasia, the order of disappearance is the inverse. The rarest phonemes are the first to disappear.

In the following section of his work, Jakobson extends his theory to two applications:

(a) The language of dreams: For Jakobson, the degenerate [dégradé] language that one uses in dreams follows the same differentiations as the language of aphasiacs. One can observe the same alterations there: rare phonemes disappear first, leaving only the most elementary phonemes. This will explain the equivocal in dream thought, which will be either parallel to that of language, or derived from it.

(b) Application: It is again according to the rules of the phonemic system that Jakobson explains what happens when someone is looking for a word: the scheme which remains in memory is incapable of realizing itself in terms of one word, because the phonemic system is differentiated at least in this respect.

These two extensions of Jakobson's theory elucidate for us the nature of the phonemic system.

2. *Originality of phonological analysis.* The originality of phonological analysis (Trubetzkoy, Jakobson) comes from what they consider to be anterior to language, in a sense, above language. Language is a system of signs linked to significations. The problem is to see the relationship between the sign and the signification. The phonologist, as such, studies the vocal elements which are already signs, but which are without designatable significations. Phonemes by themselves do not mean anything; they only serve to distinguish one word from another. The phonologist brackets off the acquired language. He tries to rediscover the signs in their originary [27] function within the verbal

27. [Merleau-Ponty uses the expression *fonction originaire.* Since he has just suggested a bracketing or suspending procedure, the adjective "originary" recalls James S. Churchill's translation of *originär* in Edmund Husserl, *The Phenomenology of Internal Time-Consciousness* (Bloomington: Indiana University Press, 1964). Husserl uses this term to mean the direct essential appearance of temporal objects. Originary intentional acts reveal an object under the phenomenological attitude.]

chain, short of all the conventions or all the historical events that in the end have attributed a given meaning to a given word. According to Saussure, language is a system of signs in the process of differentiating one from the other. For the word, as for the phoneme, the phonologist looks for the differentiating modalities which correspond to differences in signification.

The phonologist studies the word as it refers to [*renvoie à*] language, the rule of sign usage. The problem is not to find out how significations are associated apart from signs, but how phonemes articulate one another, how sound cuts off the world from meaning. The whole of phonic signs shows gesticulations, movements in the world of the signified.

Language [*langage*] has a function analogous to the language [*langue*] of a new writer who, at first, is not understood, but who little by little becomes understandable by teaching people to understand him. His gestures seem to point in nonexistent directions; then, little by little, some notions begin to find for themselves a potential [*virtuel*] home in these gestures. In the same way, language ends up by coming alive for the child. At a certain moment, the whole set of indications, which draw toward an undetermined goal, call up in the child a concentration and a reassimilation of meaning. The internal structure of the language carries with it its signification. Language is a system of a limited number of unities serving to express an unlimited number of things. There is therefore a going beyond of the signifier toward the signified. The totality of meaning is never fully rendered: there is an immense mass of implications, even in the most explicit of languages; or rather, nothing is ever completely expressed, nothing exempts the subject who is listening from taking the initiative of giving an interpretation.

Trubetzkoy shows that phonemes are not atoms. He is not as concerned with studying the phenomena in themselves as he is with understanding the distinctions between them. Words in relation to phonemes can be compared to melodies in relation to tones. They are modulations of the phonemic system.

Language, he goes on to say, is a screen "utilized" by all who use this language. For example, a Russian-speaking German transforms the German according to the structure of the Russian phonemic system.

Whereas phonetics is the study of sounds as they are produced from the outside, phonology is an effort to return to the immanent reason by which sounds organize themselves in a language. At the same time that phonology studies phonemes, it also studies all the distinctive signs of a language: prosodic relations,[28] accentuations, languages that count syllables and those that do not count them.

Language has a threefold function:

(*a*) a representative function;

(*b*) an expressive function;

(*c*) a function of appealing to other people.

Phonology studies values: the values of sounds whose validity is determined according to these three relationships. The phoneme is neither a physical reality, nor a psychological reality, but a value with an abstract and fictive importance comparable to that of money. Phonemes render the existence of a language possible.

3. *How can the child acquire a phonemic system?* Jakobson tries to explain the child's appropriation of the phonemic system and how, for the child, "the self-sufficiency of isolated and unrelated sensations transforms itself into a conceptual distribution of these same elements."

A conceptual distribution would be produced in the child's mind; that is, he would understand and would start again with vocal phenomena that originally were uncoordinated. The phonetic system has to be reinvented by the child, just as it had been invented by the group [*la collectivité*]. In reality, Jakobson compromises what is original in the phonological analysis by treating the phonemic system as a conceptual system. He himself compares the acquisition of this phonemic system to the acquisition of a system of colors. Now, progress in the percep-

28. [Relations "which include accent, pitch, cadence, and pauses; they do not change the meaning of an utterance, but convey additional, concomitant information through their conventional acceptance by the speaking group." From Mario Pei, *Glossary of Linguistic Terminology* (New York: Anchor, 1966), p. 223.]

tion of colors is not a matter of intellectual analysis; it is an articulation of a *Gestaltung* of perceptions themselves.[29] Similarly, the acquisition of the phonemic system cannot result in an intellectual classification: the child assumes the range of phonemes, which are immanent to the language he hears, in the same way that he assumes the structures of the perceived world.

4. *Conclusion.* Jakobson's interpretation would be acceptable if language had only a representative function. But we have stated along with K. Bühler that language is indissolubly:

(*a*) representation;

(*b*) self-expression;

(*c*) appeal to others.[30]

The child's movement toward speech is a constant appeal to others. The child recognizes in the other another one of himself. Language is the means of effecting reciprocity with the other. This is a question of a vital operation and not only an intellectual act. The representative function is an aspect of the total act by which we enter into communication with others.

One could sum up in the notion of style what is newest in the phonological analysis. The phonemic system is a style of language. The style is defined neither by words nor by ideas; it possesses not a direct signification but an oblique one. It permits one to characterize the phonemic system of a language just as it permits one to characterize a writer.

B. *The Phenomenon of Imitation*

After the acquisition of a phonemic system and of the first words, we say that the child develops his language by imitation. We will study the problem of imitation in general before applying it to language acquisition.

1. *The classical conception.* The problem of imitation will be the following: After having seen a gesture or a word, how is the

29. See my course of December 15, 1959, entitled: *Structure et conflits de la conscience enfantine*, in *Bulletin de psychologie*, no. 236, XVIII 3–6 (Paris, 1964), 171–202.

30. Bühler, *Sprachtheorie*.

child able to take this gesture or word as a model and to produce an equivalent gesture or word? This seems to presuppose a twofold process: in order to translate a visual behavior into a motor language, one must first understand what stimulates the behavior of others and then reproduce it. In reality, this double translation does not exist. It is impossible for the child to return to the motivating and muscular causes of gestures in others, and then to reproduce these conditions. We have already seen that the phonemic system is never acquired by this double movement from effect to cause and cause to effect. As we understand it, the phonemic system is like a register of scales for the child. Consequently, that which the child hears and reproduces is not a perceptual performance [*spectacle perceptif*], but a particular usage which is determined by the surrounding phonetic possibilities. If it is truly a question of scales (Trubetzkoy), the child reproduces them without analyzing them. Analysis is a task which comes much later. Hence, imitation cannot be this task of double translation.

2. *The problem of imitation according to Guillaume.* In his thesis on imitation, Guillaume goes beyond the classical conception.

He begins with a decisive remark: before making a movement, we do not represent this movement to ourselves; we do not envision the muscular contractions necessary for effecting it. (The preliminary representation of the movement that facilitates its initiation is a pathological symptom in certain cases of paresis, for example.)

Rather, there is a certain attraction exercised by the object: the goal that we fix for ourselves. We represent for ourselves not the movement toward an object but the desired object itself. Similarly, to speak, we do not represent the sentence to ourselves before pronouncing it. It is either the words of the interlocutor or our own words that call up what follows. Furthermore, even if one wanted to represent the succession of one's movements to oneself, it would be impossible: consciousness is unaware of "the adjustments of muscles." This is especially true for the child who is totally ignorant of anatomy.

Since we are incapable of representing to ourselves our own

movements, how could we represent to ourselves the movements of someone else? We will presume, therefore, that, from now on, imitation of oneself (repetition) or of others is founded on something besides the representation of movements. However, what is the intermediary between the perception that we have of ourselves and the visual perception of others, if it is not this representation of movements?

Classical psychology has placed us in the presence of a relation with four elements, of which two are lacking (i.e., visual perception of ourselves and the kinesthetic perception of others). It tries to show how we make up for them. As for visual perception of ourselves, Guillaume has a very simple experiment showing how lacunary it is. He draws several signs on his child's neck. The child succeeds in reproducing them correctly; but when traced on his forehead, the child reproduces the mirror image of them. The classical interpretation of imitation presupposes my analysis of the motivating conditions of other people's gestures and founds itself on a preliminary identification of their attitudes and of mine. Guillaume proposes to invert the problem: that which is a preliminary condition for classical psychologists is a mere consequence for him. Instead of saying that the identification of the other's body with mine produces imitation through their twofold (kinesthetic and visual) aspect, Guillaume says that the child first imitates the result of the action by using his own means and thereby finds himself producing the same movements as those of the model.

The third term between myself and others will be the external world: the objects that are indicated by the action of others as my own.

A profound and fertile idea arises: at first, we have consciousness not of our own body but of things. There is a quasi-ignorance of the modalities of action, but the body moves toward things. Imitation is only understood as an encounter of two actions around the same object. To imitate is not to act like others, but to obtain the same result as others. At nine months and twenty-one days, Guillaume's child seized the pencil upside down and used it to hit the table, but after several tries he turned the pencil over so as to place the point on the paper. This was not a question of the child reproducing the gesticulation of his father, but rather a question of obtaining the same result as he (i.e., the position of the pencil in relation to the paper). Several weeks later, the child used the pencil no longer for hitting the table but for tracing lines on the paper. There again, he was imitating not his father's gestures but, rather, the result. It is the same situation for all the actions which the child sees accomplished around him: to which his gestures bear only an approximate and imperfect resemblance.

This means that the imitation is immanent;[31] it aims at the global result and not the detail of the gesture. The imitation of gestures arises only little by little from this behavior oriented toward things. This is the case, for example, when children (and even dogs that are accustomed to their master) turn to look in the same direction as the adult. In this behavior, there was, perhaps, originally the fact that the adult's look fell on something interesting. But soon the parallelism between the two actions became separated from their goal, and the child systematically looked in the same direction as the adult. In any case, this imitation cannot be explained by a kinesthetic imitation. When the child turns his head in the same direction as the adult, his movement is different from that of the adult in view of their different positions in relation to the same object. It seems impossible that the child could be making the transposition. The phenomenon can be explained if we acknowledge that, for the child, the adult's look indicates a goal that he adopts in turn.

31. [The term that appears in the text is *eminente*. However, we must remember that this was a course transcribed by Merleau-Ponty's students. Although he reviewed the text, it would seem that the sense of this sentence might be more accurately rendered by the phenomenological term *immanente*, which would correspond more to the global presence of the imitated result. The text does not indicate that the result is "eminent"; rather, it is the "imitation" which is characterized. One might expect Merleau-Ponty to say that the result —but not the imitation—is crucial, distinguished, or eminent for the child. The imitation is not a transposed act, one that goes outside of what is immediately lived by the child. The imitation would therefore be "immanent," personal, primordial, the lived experience of the child. See also Merleau-Ponty's use of the word "immanent" on p. 51.]

In short, one makes use of his own body not as a mass of sensations, doubled by a kinesthetic image, but as *a way of systematically* going toward objects (and as far as the look is concerned, it is a way of inspecting objects). Imitation can be explained to the extent that other people utilize the same means as we do in order to obtain the same goal; it cannot be explained otherwise. Guillaume indicates that imitation is founded on a community of goals, of objects. It is from this imitation of results that subsequently the imitation of others becomes possible. Little by little, the adult becomes the most imposing element in the world, the measure of all things. He represents for children their most essential self [*moi*]. Consequently, by partial imitations the child takes up particular representations on his own. These partial imitations are a sign that he recognizes other people in himself. Other people are the universal intermediary between the world and the child.

There is a contrast between involuntary imitations at the beginning and explicit imitation much later. Guillaume observes a child of nine months who knows how to brush his own hair and that of others with a hair brush. But twenty days later, the same child is unable to imitate the gesture of lifting his hand to his head without a brush—he is still unreceptive [*imperméable*] to the nonconcrete and aimless gesture.[32]

Guillaume also observes a child of thirty-two months who has been asked to imitate the movement of turning his eyes from one side to the other. The child begins by turning his head. This fact effectively proves that the child is imitating the result and not the means by which the model obtains these results.

As we are accustomed to understand it, imitation (that is, to intentionally sketch out a gesture with one's body) is a delayed function. It places in question not the object itself but rather a sign, an expression of the object.

In imitation, other people are first considered not as body but as behavior.

32. With this observation Guillaume anticipates or rejoins Goldstein's analyses, which distinguish between concrete behavior and categorial behavior.

3. *Application to language:* Vocal imitation is a particular case of imitation in general. But it has the advantage of being precisely controllable by hearing [*l'ouïe*]: one is always witness to his own speech. As far as the imitation of speech is concerned, one finds himself in possession of a double kinesthetic gift which is lacking in the imitation of gestures. This gives a false simplicity to the problem of language acquisition through imitation, while in reality the problem is precisely as we have posed it for imitation in general.

It is still the imitation of articulatory gestures that is in question. We can note that the child reproduces new sounds by assimilating them to those that he has already spoken. Here too, imitation signifies carrying oneself by one's own means toward a goal (heard speech). The child imitates as he goes along [*dessine*], not by following the model point by point, but by carrying himself toward a global result.

C. [*The Imitation of Other People*]

1. *Extensions of Guillaume's theory.* Before imitating other people, the child imitates the acts of other people. This initial imitation presupposes that the child grasps directly the body of others as the carrier of structured behavior [*conduites*]. It also presupposes that he experience his own body as a permanent and global power capable of realizing gestures that are endowed with a certain meaning. This means that imitation presupposes the apprehension of a behavior in other people and, on the side of the self, a noncontemplative, but motor, subject, an "I can" (Husserl).

The perception of behavior in other people and the perception of the body itself by a global *corporeal schema* are two aspects of a single organization that realizes the identification of the self with others.

(*a*) The role of identification. This role is primordial. In effect, the self and others are entities that the child dissociates only belatedly. He starts out in terms of a total identification with others.

How, out of this primitive identification with others, is he able to realize his self and his aptitude in reproducing behavior? How can we explain the appearance of imitative consciousness? And in general, how can we explain the passage from the identification to the differentiation of self and others?

Guillaume never directly answers this question, but he is constantly brought to the point of treating it obliquely. The child's imitation develops on a plane of *unconscious* egocentrism. The child is completely oriented toward others and toward things; he confuses himself with them. With his exclusive interest in the external world, he takes even that which exists only for him as reality.

It is imitation that will assist him in escaping from this undifferentiation and will render the formation of a represented self possible.

In all, Guillaume reverses the classical problem of the relation between self and others. The classical problem was a question of passing from consciousness of self to consciousness of others. For Guillaume, it is a question of constructing a representative self from others. In effect, it is other people who occupy the principal position for the child. The child considers himself only as "another other." The center of his interest is other people. The consciousness of a unique "incomparable" (Malraux) self does not exist in the child. This self is certainly lived by him, but is not thematically grasped in all cases. Other people are essential for the child. They are the mirror of himself and that to which his self is attached. As Guillaume has noted, "the self is ignorant of itself in that it is the center of the world." [33]

To confirm this thesis, Guillaume invokes the testimony of language.

(*b*) Confirmation by language. The child's egocentrism reflects itself in the development of language: the confusion of pronouns, the predominance of other people's names over his own, etc. There is a total lack of division between self and others, but if one of these terms had a privileged signification, it would probably be others.

i. The first words of the child concern other people, as much

33. See Guillaume, *Imitation in Children*, p. 151.

and more than himself. They prove that his consciousness is consciousness not for the self [*pour soi*],[34] but rather *with others* (the expression "no more," used by all children, signifies: I don't want any more, he doesn't want anymore, there is no more, etc.).[35] Even affective expressions like *bobo* [36] principally serve to express objective realities.

ii. Similarly, the delayed appearance of the use of his own name indicates the primordial importance of other people. It is used much later than the names of the people around him. When he finally makes use of his own name, it is above all to mark his place beside others (for example, in a distribution). The evolution of pronouns is equally tardy, marking the persistence of the confusion between self and other people. "I" is used long after "you," and "he" is replaced by the first name, which is not abandoned until near the end of the second year.

Does the acquisition of these words play the role of effect or cause in relation to the consciousness of self? There is evidently a reciprocal action; the word defines the notion. But the child would not know how to understand the meaning of pronouns if his experience did not already involve reciprocity with other people.

Language is only a particular case of imitation. Guillaume compares the acquisition of a new word with the adoption of a

34. [In European philosophy since Hegel's *für sich*, the notion of the *pour-soi* is a recurrent issue. It is particularly central to Sartre's writings in the forties, where it is distinguished from the *en-soi* (*an sich*) or "in-itself." The *pour-soi* is usually translated as "for-itself." Hence, we find the third part of Merleau-Ponty's *Phenomenology of Perception* translated as "Being-for-itself and Being-in-the-World" (*Etre-pour-soi et l'être-au-monde*). We may therefore assume that although the *pour-soi* here is more appropriately translated as "for the self," the French reader's association with the *pour-soi* as a term for consciousness would be significant.]

35. [Merleau-Ponty refers to the French expression *a plus*, which signifies *je n'en veut plus, il n'en veut plus, il n'y en a plus*, etc. The translation offered above is to approximate the French expression. An American child would probably be more apt to say "all gone" signifying: "mine is all gone," "his is all gone," "there is no more in the house," etc.]

36. *Bobo* is a word used by children meaning a minor physical hurt.

role: to borrow a new expression, like borrowing a new suit, is a form of behavior.

(c) Analysis of affective imitation. What is of interest in imitation is that it is oriented much more toward other people than toward acts, i.e., the imitation of sentiments, emotions, etc. . . . is practically as precocious as that of acts. Thus, imitation constitutes a kind of stumbling-block for Guillaume's theory, and this analysis permits him to correct his conceptions somewhat. For if it is true that both are equally precocious, then the imitation of acts ought to involve a human component instead of an interest in the object alone.

There exists in the child a concern for the feelings of other people. It is not a question of the contagiousness of emotions, the invasion of other people's emotions, which one can also find in animals. Here it is a kind of egocentric sympathy, the child's participation in the sentiments of others. It is never an irresistible participation: it occupies the child fully for an instant, but he detaches himself just as quickly, with a kind of indifference that astonishes the adult. The true sympathy is not this contagiousness. It is rather a momentary enlarging of his own life: it consists of living for a moment in other people, and not only in living the same thing as others for his own benefit. Thus, when the child sees the maid being punished, he cries and *seeks refuge beside her;* it is himself that the child pities. True sympathy is a momentary investment in others to the point of encompassing others. The child will have to pass from primitive sympathy to real sympathy by a movement analogous to that which carries him from the imitation of acts or results to imitation per se, that is, to the imitation of men.

For Guillaume, this passage occurs in play. This is the function by which child and parents exchange roles for the first time. The child changes perspective. By that act, he learns to distinguish other people from himself [*autrui de soi*]. Guillaume cites the Scandinavian author Finnbogason, who had published a book on imitative intelligence in 1913.[37] The central idea is that of

37. Guomundur Finnbogason, *L'Intelligence sympathique*, trans. André Courmont (Paris: Alcan, 1913).

accommodation, which allows true imitation. When one partially imitates the behavior of others, one is obliged, by a kind of induction, to take on the total attitude corresponding to that behavior. For example, one automatically takes on the voice of the person whose gestures one is imitating. When one adopts an aspect of other people's behavior, the totality of consciousness takes on "the style" of the person who is being imitated. In other words, true imitation permeates beyond conscious limits and becomes global: once it has been *accommodated,* imitation supercedes itself. It is this kind of superceding [*dépassement*] that permits the appropriation of new structures and, for example, the acquisition of language.

In his thesis on imitation, Guillaume makes use of two very important notions, but he refuses to analyze them further. They are:

i. the notion of a pre-self, of a latent ego [*moi*], which remains in ignorance of itself because it has not yet encountered in others a limit to the self. According to Guillaume, this notion remains inaccessible to analysis because of the undifferentiation appropriate to this stage of the development of consciousness.

ii. the movement that carries the child toward others and allows him to pass from the imitation of acts to the imitation of persons. Guillaume explains this passage only as a "transfer" (an associationist notion that transforms this displacement into an illusion).

We cannot avoid the analysis of these notions, which imply the whole problem of other people. The relation with others, as Guillaume conceives it in imitation, presupposes a quasi-magical relationship with our own body and the acts of others which are perceived by us as melodic totalities (to the extent that we have the same capacities).

These are the notions that the phenomenology of Husserl and Scheler has tried to submit to a philosophical elucidation.

2. *The problem of other people's existence according to Husserl.*[38]

38. See principally the Fifth Cartesian Meditation. [In Edmund Husserl, *Cartesian Meditations,* trans. Dorion Cairns (The Hague: Nijhoff, 1960).]

(*a*) Posing the problem: the apparent impossibility of having a conception of others. The Cartesian *cogito* poses the problem of self [*moi*] and others in terms that seem to render a solution impossible. In effect, if the mind or the self were to define itself by its contact with itself, how could the representation of other people be possible? The self only has signification insofar as it is consciousness of self. Everything can be doubted by him except for the fact that he thinks; everything can be doubted except for the fact that he sees; etc. All experience presupposes contact with oneself. All knowledge is possible only by this primary knowledge. Other people will be a self which appears to me from without; this is contradictory.

It is repugnant to the other, by definition, to be only the consciousness that I have of him, since he is for himself [*pour soi*] what I am for me [*pour moi*], and for this reason I cannot have access to him. Since others are not for me what they are for themselves, I have no experience of others. Even if I wanted, by a kind of spiritual sacrifice, to renounce my *cogito* in order to posit that of others, it would still be from me that he would have this existence, and by which he would still be *my* phenomenon.

The relationship between self and others appears therefore to be a relationship of reciprocal exclusion. And the problem appears to be insoluble.

(*b*) Existence of the phenomenon of other people. The phenomenon of other people, however, is unchallengeable. A large number of our attitudes and behaviors are understandable only as a function of others. We have experience of other people even if it is not certain that it is according to the manner of our experience of ourselves. (As Husserl has said, a certain solipsism is insurmountable.) The problem is therefore that one must posit others (which seems logically impossible), since for all practical purposes other people do exist.

The solution: to transform this relation of exclusion into a living relation.

The givens of the problem are: one must admit a certain presence of others, but an indirect presence, since the only indubitable presence is myself (a requirement of the *cogito*).

Husserl seeks a number of ways to attain the perception of others:

i. "Lateral" perception: Other people never exist in front of me in the fashion of objects, but they always imply a certain "orientation," a reference in relation to me [*moi*]. He is the alter ego, a kind of reflection for me. It is not a question of conceiving of a series of "for-itself's [*pour-soi*], but a community of alter egos, existing for each other. Others take their existence, in a certain sense, from me.

ii. "Lacunary" perception: We perceive other people in relation to ourselves simultaneously as a reflection and as a lack. In effect, it is like a forbidden zone in our experience.

It is precisely a question of a real *perception* of other people (in the sense of unchallengeable experience; others are present "in person"), but it is not the same kind of perception that we have of objects. As far as objects are concerned, that which is not actually given to me could always exist as such virtually (from another point of view, in the microscope, etc.). As far as other people are concerned, it will always be impossible for us to perceive them in their totality, in the same way in which they perceive themselves.

There is a limit to presence "in the flesh": we never occupy exactly the same place as others. By definition, if we were in their place, we would be them (the distinction between our position, *hic,* and theirs, *illic*).

In considering both lateral perception and lacunary perception, we have not yet really posited other people. I must go beyond, truly penetrate their field, if I want to fully affirm the existence of others.

iii. Perception of other people's behavior. Here, Husserl's analysis is completely parallel to that of Guillaume. When I witness the setting in of the behavior of others, my body becomes a means of understanding them, my corporality becomes a comprehending power of their corporality—I regain the final meaning (the *Zwecksinn*) of other people's behavior, because my body is capable of achieving the same goals. There the notion of style intervenes: because the style of my gestures and the gestures of others is the same, this amounts to the fact that what is true for me is also true for others. "Style" is not a concept, an idea: it is a "manner" that I apprehend and then imitate, even if I am unable [*hors d'état*] to *define* it.

iv. Intentional transfer.[39] The operation of conceiving other people's existence is more than a perception of their style. It must be like a pairing (*Paarung*): a body encountering its counterpart in another body which itself realizes its own intentions and suggests new intentions to the self [*moi*]. The perception of others is the assumption of one organism by another. Husserl gives a number of names to this vital operation which gives us the experience of others while transcending our own self. He calls it "intentional transfer" or "apperceptive transfer," while always insisting on the fact that it is not a logical operation that is in question (*kein Schluss, kein Denkakt*"), but rather a vital one.[40] The behavior of others conforms to my own intentions to such an extent, and designates a behavior which has so much meaning for me, that it is as though I assume it.

3. *Husserl's position.* To what extent does Husserl find a solution to the problem of the existence of other people in the context of an intuitive philosophy? There is, as we have said and as he has said, a fundamental contradiction: the experience of other people is given to us, but we cannot posit it logically. It is a question of rendering explicit the existence of other people. This seems impossible, given the primordial condition which Husserl does not intend to abandon and which, on the contrary, he recalls each time we would believe him to be on the verge of a solution. This condition is the Cartesian conception of the *cogito*:

39. ["Transfer" is the English rendering of the French word *transgression*. However, Merleau-Ponty seems to be discussing what Husserl called *intentionale Modifikation* in § 52 of the *Cartesianische Meditationen* (The Hague: Nijhoff, 1950). Merleau-Ponty might be referring, therefore, to what Dorion Cairns translates as "intentional modification." In the course of his discussion, Merleau-Ponty refers to what he claims Husserl calls *transgression intentionelle* or *transposition apperceptive*. This latter is clearly Husserl's *apperzeptive Übertragung*, which occurs in § 50 and which Dorion Cairns renders as "apperceptive transfer."]

40. [*Apperzeption ist kein Schluss, kein Denkakt*" appears in § 50 of the *Cartesianische Meditationen*. Dorion Cairns translates it as "Apperception is not inference, not a thinking act."]

the experience of others ought to be conceived as another self. Without the alter ego, Husserl states, there is no other organism.

In that way, he denies the pseudosolution that would consist of accepting the existence of other people's consciousness as beginning with my own and as verifying the analogy between our behaviors. There is conflict here with Descartes' dichotomy between extension and thought: how can we relate one to the other? This is the problem of relating the order of the in-itself [en-soi] to the order of the for-itself [pour-soi]. The other is a for-itself that appears to me in things, through a body, hence in the in-itself. To conceive of this passage, one would have to elaborate a mixed notion, which would be unthinkable for Descartes. Husserl also refuses to supercede the constitutive contradiction in the perception of other people. I cannot allow myself to be reduced to the image that other people have of me. Thus, since I am not successful in positing myself from the perspective of other people, neither can I pretend to posit other people from my own perspective.

Having shown the impossibility of surmounting this contradiction and the impossibility of a synthesis, Husserl adds that this synthesis is not what is needed, and that the problem is poorly posed. The difference between my point of view and the point of view of others only exists after we have experienced other people. It is a consequence; as he states, we must not posit this distinction at the outset and then oppose it to every conception of the experience of others. But, with this remark, it seems that Husserl wants to reject the idea that one attains the experience of others by starting with the consciousness of self. He seems to be orienting himself in another direction. Thus, there are two tendencies in this work:

(a) the attempt to gain access to others by starting with the cogito, with the "sphere of ownness"; [41]

(b) the denial of this problem and an orientation toward "intersubjectivity," that is, the possibility of starting without

41. [Merleau-Ponty's sphère d'appartenance is here rendered by Cairn's "sphere of ownness." Husserl called it Eigenheitssphäre (Cartesianische Meditationen, § 49).]

positing the primordial *cogito,* starting with a consciousness which is neither self nor others.

But while envisaging this second possibility, Husserl effectively shows that, even though it would be satisfactory, it does not hide the difficulties of the problem which remain intact for him. Thus, at the frontier of an intersubjective conception, Husserl finally maintains an integral transcendental subjectivity.

Later, Husserl was even more conscious of the problem and came to the point of affirming the two requirements simultaneously. For example, he says, in his unpublished writings, that transcendental subjectivity *is* intersubjectivity (the experience that other people have of me validly teaches me that which I am). But he is not able to reconcile the two.

(4). *Max Scheler's view.*[42] Scheler, a student of Husserl, tries to find a solution to the problem and to secure the perception of others by completely renouncing the *cogito* from the start (that is, by abandoning the Cartesian postulate that consciousness is primarily consciousness of self). He begins explicitly with the total *undifferentiation* between self and other people.

He generalizes the notion of "inner perception" (the perception of feelings, for example), which applies as much to other people as to oneself. On the one hand, the perception of my own body or of my own behavior is as external as, and no more immediate than, the perception of objects. On the other hand, we see, we perceive the feelings of others (not only their expression); we perceive them with the same certitude as our own feelings. The differences between the diverse feelings are provided by the perception itself. For example, it is impossible to confuse in other people the redness of shame with that of anger, heated arousal, etc. Perception takes us a long way into the comprehension of other people.[43] There is the perception of the will of others as well; sometimes we even perceive it as our own will, etc. It would be necessary to speak of a "current of

42. Max Scheler, *The Nature of Sympathy,* trans. Peter Heath (New Haven, Conn.: Yale University Press, 1954).

43. Cf. Proust: the discernment of Albertine's lie. [Marcel Proust, *Remembrance of Things Past,* trans. C. K. Scott-Moncrieff and Frederick A. Blossom (New York: Random House, 1932).]

undifferentiated psychic experience," a mixture of self and others, primitive consciousness in a kind of generality, a state of permanent "hysteria" (in the sense of an indistinctness between that which is lived and that which is only imagined between self and others).

How does the consciousness of self emerge from this indistinctness? Scheler says that one has a consciousness of self only through expression (acts, reactions, etc.)—one takes on consciousness of self as he does of others, in the same way that intentions are only known once they are realized.[44]

Thus, consciousness of self cannot be given a privileged position. It is impossible without consciousness of others. It is of the same variety. Like all experience, the experience of self exists only as a figure against a ground. (Perception of others is like the ground from which perception of self separates itself.) We see ourselves through the intermediary of others.

But a problem remains: for Husserl, the problem is to go from consciousness of self to that of others. In Scheler's view, it is a question of understanding how the consciousness of self and of others can arise out of a background of primitive indistinctness.

5. *Discussion of Scheler.* For Max Scheler, *consciousness is inseparable from its expression* (consequently, it is inseparable from the cultural whole of its milieu). There is *no radical difference between consciousness of self and consciousness of other people.*

But does that make it clear how the subject comes to posit *other people?* How is there an isolation and a plurality of consciousnesses?

To this Scheler answers: consciousnesses are only separate through their corporality, through the whole set of instruments that they use. "Corporality" is, in a way, the sensible matter that assists in the apprehension of oneself or of others. But the purely sensible aspect of a feeling constitutes only a minor portion of it. All the rest, its content, its *intention,* can be shared with other

44. Cf. Alain [Emile Auguste Chartier], *Propos sur la Peinture,* Vols. I–II (Paris: Gallimard, 1956).

people. Thus, in a fire, only the subject who is burned can feel the sensible sharpness of the pain. But everything that the burn represents: the menace of fire, the danger for the well-being of the body, the *signification of the pain,* can be communicated to other people and felt by other people. It is therefore the same form, the same content which is lived through another channel [*matière*]. The signification, the intuition of the feeling (that which constitutes its essentials) is the same for the two consciousnesses. There is an isolation of the *felt* [*senti*], but not an isolation of consciousnesses.

Scheler introduces the notion of *emotional evidence.* One cannot become the other *really,* but one can become him intentionally. One can reach others through all the expressive manifestations by which they give themselves to us. There is no split in our consciousness of other people (the perception of the manifestations of others involves a hypothesis about their consciousness—by analogy with our own consciousness, which produces similar manifestations). With others as with ourselves, consciousness and its manifestations are one.

Husserl had posed the problem in terms of consciousness. That is what rendered it unsolvable. Scheler tried to pose the problem in terms of *individuality.*

Scheler's essential contribution is the notion of *expression.* There is no consciousness *behind* the manifestations. These manifestations are inherent in consciousness; they *are* consciousness. It is because other people are completely whole in their manifestations that I can posit them: by their very existence and not by analogical reasoning.

So as to render the consciousness of other people possible, Scheler minimizes consciousness of self. He reduces it to a simple contact with one's self. This contact realizes itself little by little through experience and is never achieved; it never becomes a full possession of self. In this conception, the *cogito* takes on an importance that is generalizable, applicable to others as well as to oneself. The *cogito,* in the Cartesian sense, is undeniably a conquest of culture. Since it has given rise to a coming to consciousness [*prise de conscience*], it is not primordial. Since it was subordinated to a whole series of cultural conditions that permitted this coming to consciousness of self [*prise de conscience de soi*], as with all consciousness, it appears under the guise of *expression*.

With Husserl, there was already a tendency to revise the notion of the *cogito* (the incarnation of the self in its expressions). But this tendency clashed with the very definition of a pure consciousness. With Scheler, consciousness is opaque, completely invested in its expressions. But is not a coming to consciousness of self, and of others as alter egos, rendered impossible in this way? Does he not equate consciousness of self with that of others on the level of a neutral psychism which is neither one nor the other? Even with the introduction of "emotional evidence," we know only behaviors and not persons. In pain, for example, one does not perceive other people, as long as one does not represent to himself their material and sensible pain. The intentional element of the feeling is only a generality in relation to the true feeling. One does not have a real experience of other people, as long as one has not linked the significations of a feeling to the very fact of *living these significations*. Scheler's view skirts a kind of panpsychism, at the heart of which there is no individuation of consciousnesses. How can a subject who will not be a consciousness of self (in the Husserlian sense of the term) emerge as the subject of this common stream?

D. *Conclusions*

1. In minimizing consciousness of self, Scheler equally compromises consciousness of others. Husserl, on the contrary, wanting to retain the originality of the ego, cannot introduce other people except as destroyers of this ego. With Husserl, as with Scheler, the ego and other people are linked by the same dialectical relation. While they seem to exclude one another, they are bizarrely allied; in the end, it is impossible to save one at the expense of the other: both vary in the same sense.[45]

45. Cf. the relation between master and slave in the Hegelian dialectic. [See G. W. F. Hegel, *The Phenomenology of Mind*, trans. J. B. Baillie (New York: Harper, 1931), pp. 228–40. This occurs in the section on "Self-Consciousness."]

Hence, to solve the problem, one must not eliminate the initial opposition. Theoretically, it is insurmountable. However, since it is not a logical relation but an existential one, the self could rejoin other people by rendering the *lived experience* more profound. The self must become bound up with certain *situations*. We must link the very notion of ipseity to that of situation: the ego ought to be defined as identical with the act in which it projects itself. The self and others are conscious of one another in a common situation. It is in this sense that we must clarify Scheler's view and Husserl's notion of "pairing." At issue is an encounter within the same orientation. But, at the same time, there is no possibility of understanding, except in the *present* (a kind of geometrical locus for the self and others) and in an *assignable reality*.

When Malraux says "One dies alone, therefore one lives alone," he is making a false deduction. Life, in fact, radically surpasses individualities, and it is impossible to judge it in relation to death, which is an individual failure.[46]

2. As we have seen, the conception of consciousness, in

46. [In Jacquet's notes for Merleau-Ponty's 1947–48 course on Language and Communication at the University of Lyon, we find the following passage:

Language is two consciousnesses placed in communication by an inert medium. Without a doubt, I am alone in the fact of suffering and death; but is this a normal relation or is it a decomposition of the normal? It seems that in the face of death, the true essence of consciousness does not seem to express itself. Malraux has said incorrectly that "one dies alone, therefore one lives alone." In life, the essence of consciousness is communication, where one cannot determine what is ours and what belongs to others. Our perception of others is a modification of ourselves. Man is a sorcerer for man. We are coresponsible for what the other does. What is in question is to know whether the insularity of consciousness must not be placed in doubt. We must describe our relations with others before having reflected. In life, there is the zone of the voluntary, of the reflected knowing, but before that there is the prepersonal zone. This first level perhaps motivates my whole being. The true *cogito* is not to say: I have sensations or universal conceptual thoughts, but it is this experience of a view which, in principle, is open toward others even if it is not yet known by others. Thus [the *cogito*] is through the sensible itself, and never the experience of a movement toward others. One must therefore represent the relations with others to oneself before reflection.]

Scheler's perspective and even in certain passages from Husserl, refers us to *expression,* which is considered as the very act by which consciousness is realized. It seems that we have thus accomplished a kind of circle: in order to understand the acquisition of language, we have studied imitation only to discover, following Guillaume, that imitation is not preceded by a coming to consciousness of other people and an identification with them; it is on the contrary the act by which identification with other people is produced. This has brought us to inquire what consciousness of oneself, and of others who accomplish this act, might be. It is in this fashion that we have found ourselves led back to the notion of expression.

But, in fact, this notion is no longer exactly the one with which we started: it has been enriched. At the outset, we considered language as an intellectual operation of deciphering other people's thought and as an intermediary between the person who speaks and he who listens. But according to this conception, the subject who learns to speak can only find the concepts that he already possesses in language. Language can add nothing new, since it presupposes thought. However, experience shows that language has as much influence on thought as the inverse. The classical notion of language, therefore, cannot account for the learning of language [*son apprentissage*].

On the contrary, in the light of Husserl's and Scheler's conceptions, we no longer can consider language acquisition as the intellectual operation of reconstructing meaning. We are no longer in the presence of two entities (expression and meaning), the second of which might be hidden behind the first. As a phenomenon of expression, language is constitutive of consciousness. From this perspective, to learn to speak is to coexist more and more with the environment. Living in this environment incites the child to recapture language and thought for his own means. Thus, acquisition no longer resembles the decoding of a text for which one possesses the code and key; rather, it is a deciphering (where the decipherer does not know the key to the code). The decipherer helps himself in two converging ways:

(*a*) by an internal critique of the text (frequency of certain signs, their arrangement, words, if there are any), that is, its structure;

(*b*) by an external criticism (place and time of the writing, situation of the writer).

It is a fact that up till now texts of all types have been deciphered. There is always an intuitive element that intervenes in this operation, since the givens of the problem never suffice to determine it logically. It is a creative operation, comparable to the learning of language by the child, in the sense that, at a given moment, the decipherer, like the child, ought to go beyond the given elements in order to grasp the significance of the whole. This is the moment in which the totality of signs, the style of the text, can no longer mean anything but one single thing, where, as Jakobson has said about a phonemic system, *it tends toward signification*.

Between the period when the child does not understand and the instant when he does understand, there is a discontinuity that is impossible to overlook. Classical psychology, in affirming that thought precedes expression, tries to cover up this gap [*hiatus*], but by the same token it takes away all the meaning of the phenomenon. In fact, just as the child learns to know himself through others, he learns to know others through himself; he also learns to speak because the surrounding language calls up his thought, because he is enticed by its style until a single meaning emerges from the whole. This is why Ombredane could call language a "semeiological gesticulation," which is to say that the meaning is immanent to living speech as it is immanent to the gestures by which we point out objects.[47]

It is necessary to compare this process to Wolff's research concerning the apprehension of an individual's style.[48] Wolff

47. [See, for example, André Ombredane, *Le Langage: Nouveau traité de psychologie*, Vol. 3 (Paris: Dumas, 1938). Also, André Ombredane, *L'Aphasie et l'elaboration de la pensée explicite* (Paris: Presses Universitaires de France, 1931).]

48. [See W. Wolff, "Selbstbeurteilung und Fremdbeurteilung in wissentlichen und unwissentlichen Versuch," *Psychologische Forschung*, XVI (1932). Merleau-Ponty had already discussed Wolff's findings in *The Structure of Behavior*, p. 157.]

shows photographs of different people to subjects who have never been initiated into the scientific disciplines. He presents them with signatures, silhouettes, and the recorded voices of the same people. He asks them to match up all these materials. The proportion of correct matches (about 70 percent) is amazing, without the subjects being able to indicate what guided them in their selection. We must admit that perception of other people grasps a unique structure, in which all their expressions, voices, writing, etc., participate. Wolff therefore gives evidence for the existence of fluent, nonthematic signification. Arising from signification of this variety, language is pregnant for the child when he hears it used around him. Hazy at first, the signification articulates itself and becomes more and more precise. It is not a question of a phenomenon on the level of pure thought or understanding. It is the *value of use* that defines language. Instrumental usage precedes signification per se. It does not occur otherwise, even at the level of the most elaborate language, for example, in the introduction of a new concept in philosophical language. It is according to his own usage that the author forces the acceptance of the sense [*sens*] in which he uses a new term. The signification that he proposes is therefore an *open* signification, without which there would be no acquisition on the level of thought. An entirely defined language (an algorithm like that of *logical positivism*) would be sterile.[49]

3. Up to now, we have considered language acquisition only in terms of the child's first words. The child has acquired the means of designating objects in their absence; but only objects that can offer themselves to sensible experience have been considered.

The same problem again poses itself on the level of "thoughts," when it has been resolved at the level of the sensible. This is what Piaget calls the "developmental lag" [*décalage*]: i.e., all that is acquired at a certain level must be started over again at a higher level. As far as the child's egocentrism is concerned, it will have been surpassed long ago on the level of per-

49. [Merleau-Ponty uses the English "logical positivism" in the text.]

ception by the time that the child has to surpass it again on the intellectual and logical plane. Moreover, even for the adult, the expression of what is most personal [*sien*] in his experience will always have to be perfected. It is in this sense that Malraux could say in his *Psychology of Art*, "How many years does an artist need before he can finally speak with his own voice." [50]

Far from being limited to the first years, language acquisition is coexistensive with the very exercise of language.

[V] Evolution of Language to Seven Years

We now return to the study of language at the point where the child has learned to designate objects in the sensible world. In order to follow the further evolution of language, we will base our discussion on Piaget's work entitled: *The Language and Thought of the Child*.[51]

Until about age seven, language, for the child, is more a means of self-expression than of communication with other people. It is *egocentric language*. One of its manifestations is the phenomenon of echolalia.

A. *The Phenomenon of Echolalia*

Echolalia is the indefinite repeating of the same word, correctly characterized by Piaget as a playful activity. The child amuses himself by his ability to produce or to verify the signification of a word by repeating it. As with play in general—which consists of adopting different roles—language as play allows the child to gain access to more and more numerous situations. By repeating the word, the child extends his behavior. He amuses himself by utilizing language as a manifestation of imaginary life.

50. [See André Malraux, *The Psychology of Art*, trans. Stuart Gilbert, 3 vols. (New York: Pantheon, 1949–50).]

51. Jean Piaget, *The Language and Thought of the Child*, trans. Marjorie Gabain (Cleveland: Meridian, 1955).

As with all play, there is the problem of knowing to what extent the child believes in the reality of these imaginary situations. In Diderot's *The Paradox of Acting*, does the actor believe that he is the character whom he is representing, or is he lying? [52] But Sartre, in *The Psychology of Imagination*, shows that a false question is being considered: [53] the child, like the actor, neither feigns nor is in illusion; he leaves the plane of daily life for a dreamlike life in which he really lives. He renders himself unreal in the role.

B. *Monologue*

Another aspect of "egocentric language" is monologue. In the presence of others, there is "collective monologue." Two or more children, while appearing to be answering one another, are in reality only pursuing their own monologues, without taking into account the reactions of the others.

The following question has been asked: does monologue precede speech with others or the inverse? Piaget has answered that for the child there is no difference between self and others (this is precisely the nature of the child's egocentrism). He believes that his thoughts and his sentiments are universal. His manner of expressing himself is therefore impersonal, anonymous ("one" addresses himself to X). The child is possessed by language, more than he possesses it. Thus, he is less closed in on himself than the adult, who is conscious of his personality, and at the same time less socialized than the adult, who, knowing how to conduct himself in the presence of other individuals, really tries to communicate with them and thinks in terms of other people even when he is alone. Thus, the surpassing of childlike egocentrism will be characterized, not by a "departure outside of oneself" (the child does not know the individual self), but by a modification of the relationship between self and others.

52. Denis Diderot, *The Paradox of Acting*, trans. Walter H. Pollock (New York: Hill & Wang, 1957).
53. [J.-P. Sartre, *The Psychology of Imagination*, trans. Bernard Frechtman (New York: Washington Square Press, 1948).]

C. *The Passage from Monologue to Dialogue*

Piaget has found that 5 to 15 percent of the child's language between five and six years consists of egocentric propositions. He distinguishes two successive stages in the development of dialogue. Whenever there is agreement of opinion between two children, the stages take the following forms:

(1) an intermediary phase, where the interlocutor is associated with an action but does not really collaborate; later, in the same phase, there is partial collaboration concerning facts or precise memories;

(2) after seven years, when there is real dialogue, discussion, and search for explanations.

When there is disagreement, we find:

(1) a pure and simple dispute or collision of nonmotivated affirmations;

(2) after about seven years, a collision of motivated affirmations and rational discussion.

But is Piaget's interpretation legitimate? He dismisses all of children's answers to adults as being non-spontaneous (from 14 to 18 percent of total speech before seven years). But what does he mean by "spontaneous"? It is a fact that the child has a different language when he is addressing an adult, but is it less spontaneous? *Anticipations*, abrupt changes to a higher level, are perhaps characteristic of childhood throughout the course of its development. (This can be compared to the notion of "prematuration" which, according to Lacan, characterizes the child's psychological development).[54] Perhaps Piaget excludes an essential element of children's language as non-"spontaneous," especially since he has pointed out that the child is silently interested in abstract notions before seven years. If one had to consider as "spontaneous" only those reactions of the child in relation to other children, one could arbitrarily lay out a picture of childhood.

54. [See, for example, Jacques Lacan, "Le Stade du miroir comme formateur de la fonction du Je" (1949), in *Écrits* (Paris: Seuil, 1966), pp. 93–100.]

But this conception of the child's language corresponds with Piaget's general conception of childhood: he envisions it solely in terms of its provisional, and hence, negative, aspect. His conception of adult language, an ideal which the child must wait for, appears to be a narrow one. Piaget attributes only a communicative function to language.[55] The narrowness of his conceptions is reflected in the role that he attributes to *discussion*. For Piaget, when there is discussion, there is the possibility of separating out an objective truth. But we must not forget that there are other possible conceptions of discussion. Political discussion, for example, intervenes precisely at the moment when a general conception of history is applied to ambiguous facts, resulting in a lack of *objective* truth. Even in Plato's dialogues, discussion has a function which is different from that which Piaget assigns to it. Discussion contributes to the formation of truth. It is that which gives its meaning to the conclusion. It is a path toward a truth which has no meaning except in this movement, which, therefore, is not objective in Piaget's sense.

Thus, Piaget eliminates from adult language all that is self-expression and appeal to other people. However, even the power of a writer resides more in his "style" than in the communication of objective truths.[56] So we will have to find out whether the model of objectivity proposed by Piaget can serve as a measure of the givens in human language.

But it is evident that the style of the writer is not the same as that egocentric language of the child which must be surpassed. The child must pass through a stage of objective expression, even if later poetic language may resemble the child's language. It is a question of distinguishing, as in the child's drawings, an infrarational plan from an overrational plan. In the case of drawings, as in the case of verbal expression, the

55. For Bühler, in his *Sprachtheorie*, language is as much a function of self-expression and of appeal to other people as a communication of truths.

56. [An incomplete sentence—due to an apparent typesetting error—appears in the original 1964 edition. This sentence has been eliminated from a more recent printing. The incomplete sentence would read as follows: ". . . without limiting them by lending them a certain tone [*voix*] which they themselves cannot deny."]

child is not an artist. But if one admits to this metaobjective language, then the child and the adult are less foreign to one another than it would seem at first. The passage to objective language can be considered equally well as an *impoverishment.* Passing from childhood to adulthood will be not only a question of a passing from ignorance to knowledge, but also, after a phase of polymorphism in which all the possibilities were inherent, a passing to a purified language, more definite, but less rich.

[VI] COMMUNICATION BETWEEN CHILDREN OVER SEVEN

PIAGET'S EXPERIMENTS consist of controlling the transmission of a story or the explanation of a mechanism from one child to another. According to an established text, the adult recounts a story, or explains the functioning of a machine (e.g., a faucet or a syringe), to one child (called the "explainer"). Then, the explainer transmits it to the second child, the "reproducer," who must reproduce for the adult what he has understood.

A. [*Procedures*]

There are two procedures:

1. The explainer repeats his explanation once to the adult before transmitting it to the second child. (This procedure has the advantage of controlling the explanation, but there is also the disadvantage that the second explanation may not be as good, since the child is tired.)

2. The first child goes immediately to find the second, and then the second transmits to the adult what he has understood.

Piaget has established four coefficients characterizing the totality of the relationships between expression and comprehension:

(1) that which the reproducer has understood—in relation to that which the explainer has understood;

(2) that which the reproducer has understood—in relation to that which the explainer has expressed;

(3) that which the explainer has understood—in relation to what the adult has expressed;

(4) that which the explainer has expressed—in relation to that which, he, the explainer, has understood.

B. *Results*

1. The explanation of physical mechanisms is better understood than that of stories. With regard to the stories, the child understands the adult better; children understand each other poorly, but express themselves well.

2. As to the explanation of a mechanical gadget, the phenomenon is understood better than the story, but is not as well expressed.

3. In the case of gadgets, the second child understands the first one better than the first child has understood the adult in spite of the poor expression.

C. *Interpretation*

As far as the explanation of a gadget is concerned, for Piaget the best understanding comes from the fact that true communication is not in question. The second child understands the first one better because he had the gadget (or drawing) in front of him. He looks more at the object than he listens to the explainer. Everything happens as if the first child believes that he has understood more than he has in reality, and as if the second child already knew in advance what the first child was explaining to him. The words which they use are only signals which awaken the schemes that the listener already possesses. In fact, in the case of the gadgets communication is not as good as in the case of the stories; but the result is on the whole better, because the process is only based in part on the verbal transmission.

Piaget *concludes that there is no true communication between children*. In a general way, the child believes that he is explaining, while at the same time he forgets all the details. The other child understands in relation to what he already knows and believes that he understands everything. *It is rare that the child is conscious of not having understood* (5 percent). It sometimes occurs that the child who is explaining a mechanism does not even specify which mechanism is in question (faucet or syringe). He disrupts the logical, causal, and temporal order by going directly to the facts without investigating the causes. There is a reversal of the *"because";* the child uses it to attach cause to effect and not the inverse.[57] All this is part of the *verbal syncretism* (the global seizure of a phenomenon; the description only skirts around it), to be compared to the *synthetic incapacity* which Luquet reveals in children's drawings.[58]

Piaget characterizes this thinking as being of an *artistic order.* The child does not really seek understanding, for he links causes with effect in a quasi-magical fashion. For the adult there is a conviction that he has understood when he thinks he can reproduce the chain from causes to effects. For the child, the autistic patient, and, in general, in all the circumstances of emotion, this is not necessary; in all of these cases the person is convinced that he has understood at once and without following the causal chain. For the child, there is no logic except in the sequence of his own thoughts. An appeal from the outside is nothing but an activation of previously acquired schemes. An accidental detail can change the course of his thought (for example, the child hears that Odysseus was awash on shore—wash, clean—and recounts that Odysseus "cleaned the shore." [59] The child proceeds by whole sentences without analyzing them.

57. [For example, the child may say "The man fell off his bicycle because he broke his arm." See Jean Piaget, *Judgement and Reasoning in the Child*, trans. Marjorie Warden (London: Routledge & Kegan Paul, 1952), p. 17.]

58. [See G.-H. Luquet, *Les Dessins d'un enfant* (Paris: Alcan, 1913).]

59. [In the French text, Merleau-Ponty's example concerns the child who hears that "Niobe" was *attaché au roc* (attached to a rock). Confusing *attaché* with *à taché* (has spotted), the child associates spotting with cleaning the rock, and recounts that *elle a lavé un caillou* (she washed a stone). Piaget's presentation of this example occurs in chap. 3, especially p. 134, of *The Language and Thought of the Child.*]

D. *Examination of Piaget's Views*

Everything that Piaget says is exact, but must we insist on the same aspects (the transitory character of the child's thought) as he does? Do we not find the same egocentric, autistic, syncretic thinking in the adult as soon as his thinking must go beyond the domain of the acquired in order to express new notions? The notion of egocentric language can be completely modified if one admits that it exists legitimately in the adult and that it can have value for *knowledge*. In effect, a new notion cannot be explained clearly at once. The terms cannot be defined in advance since they will be fully defined only by the use that one makes of them. Consequently, since the ideal or logical order can only be overturned, as it occurs in the child, the adult makes use of the "direct method," which consists of specifically supposing as known that which is unknown. (The philosophy professor, for example, is obliged to use in his first lecture terms which his students will not fully comprehend until the end of the tenth lecture, since at the first lecture all the terms are still unknown to them.)

One can relate this illusion of a fully defined language to the notion of the "understood" [*sous-entendu*] in the area of linguistics as discussed by Saussure.[60] We call what is "understood" in another language that which is not expressed, whereas it is expressed in our own language (for example: for the English phrase "the man I love," we say that the relative pronoun is understood).[61] But this is artificial, since this notion does not really exist for those who use it. In reality, there is never anything that is "fully expressed"; there are only gaps and discontinuities, of which one is not conscious in one's own language, because comprehension between individuals speaking the same language is not affected by these gaps and discontinuities.

60. [Ferdinand de Saussure, *Course in General Linguistics*, trans. Wade Baskin (New York: McGraw-Hill, 1959).]

61. [The relative pronoun cannot be omitted in French as it can in English. One must say *l'homme que j'aime*, while in English, as Merleau-Ponty notes, we can say "the man I love" instead of "the man whom I love."]

In this sense, the language of the child does not lack communicative value, and, in any case, it cannot be appreciated in relation to the supposed notion of the "fully expressed." Sometimes children understand one another, for example, as they understand that a flattened cube drawn by another child actually represents a cube.[62] As soon as a mode of expression is understood by the partner, it must be taken as *valid* at this particular level. With his global language, the child makes himself understood by the other, who plunges into his consciousness and grasps the totality of the phenomenon through the rational order of his words. This comes from the fact that, as in drawing, where children do not project the object to be represented on a single plane, in language they do not project the signification only on the plane of logical speech. One would have to study language as a lived state, that is, not the language of the logician but that by which the orator, the writer, or even the scientist makes himself understood. One would then see that in certain respects language cannot help but be "egocentric." If Piaget has overlooked this fact, it is because the two examples that he has chosen (story or mechanism) are extremes in which there is too much or too little logic. Every child over seven will understand the mechanism of the faucet both by his previous experience and by the drawing that goes along with the explanation without having heard *what has been said to him.* On the other hand, if an episode is eliminated in the story of Odysseus, no intuition could fill this gap.

The notion of comprehension entails two aspects: one which consists of grasping the meaning of a concept which in principle has been totally expressed, and another which is taken up—in a sense, discovered—from the verbal traces. Stendhal has called these verbal traces "the little true facts" which are significant as

62. See the course on children's drawings. [Merleau-Ponty may have Luquet's book in mind. However, it is more likely that he was referring to his own course entitled: *Structure et conflits de la conscience enfantine,* which appears in the same volume of the *Bulletin de psychologie* and which includes an extended discussion of children's drawings. Merleau-Ponty was offering this course at the same time as *Consciousness and the Acquisition of Language.*]

a whole. (For example, one can grasp the whole universe of the artist through a painting.)

On the whole, Piaget clearly understands egocentric language, but he only defines it negatively, without paying attention to the intermediary cases with all their nuances. This is what happens so often in psychology, where, for purposes of simplification, only peripheral and impersonal activities are retained. For example, even the Gestaltists' studies of perception, which are based on laboratory results, lack what is most personal and most significant in the exercise of perception.

Similarly in language: logical language has the relative advantage of being exact. But one loses sight of the fact that this is only one element, a dead element, of the total language.

2 / The Pathology of Language

[I] [INTRODUCTORY COMMENTS]

IT ARISES from what has already been said that *language is a surpassing (operated by the subject on the significations at his disposal) which is stimulated by the usage made of words in his environment.* Language is an act of transcending. One cannot consider it simply as a container for thought; it is necessary to see language as an instrument for conquest of self by contact with others.

We will now attempt a counterproof of these affirmations by depending upon examples borrowed from pathology.

It is impossible to know a priori what pathology will be able to offer. Only an examination of facts will serve as a basis for revealing to us the possible relationships which exist between the normal and the pathological. Nevertheless, we can separate out two notions right away:

1. *Absolute identity between the normal and the pathological.* This is the view of nineteenth-century positivists according to which human activities are determined by natural invariable laws—in the same way that a machine, even a poorly regulated one, will always obey the laws of physics. But as Husserl has noted, if a poorly regulated machine always obeys the laws of physics, it no longer obeys the laws of mathematics. Nevertheless, one might say that we cannot compare the body to a

[63]

machine constructed with an end in view. But whoever speaks of behavior, speaks of *oriented* activity. To the extent that behavior lacks a precise goal, we can speak of a failure, for example in pathological behavior, and we can affirm the existence of a distinction between the normal and the pathological.

2. *Absolute otherness* [*altérité*]. This is a conception that is equally unacceptable. Pathological behavior also has a meaning. Sickness is self-regulating. There is an establishment of an equilibrium at a level which is other than the normal level, but here a totally incomprehensible phenomenon is not in question. Maurice Blondel was not wrong when he imputed an ineffable character to the morbid immediate consciousness, *but the structure of this consciousness remains penetrable.* The normal and the pathological can be considerably enriched by the contact of one with the other.

In the presence of the patient, the doctor ought to adopt the attitude defined by Minkowski: [1] the observation of a patient is in reality a dialogue in the course of which what is "normal" and what is "pathological" are differentiated and defined respectively. One must reject dogmatic attitudes: it is a point of fact that we can understand mental disturbances as illnesses.

We will study on the one hand the phenomenon of speech in verbal hallucination and on the other hand the disintegration of language in aphasia.

[II] VERBAL HALLUCINATION [2]

ACCESS TO THE STUDY OF ILLNESS has remained masked for quite a while by a long series of prejudices. Classical ontology, founded on the absolute distinction between the material body, the soul situated inside this body, and the external environment playing the role of stimulus, in effect, resulted in turning scientists from the study of verbal hallucination. From the moment

1. See Eugène Minkowski, *Lived Time*, trans. Nancy Metzel (Evanston, Ill.: Northwestern University Press, 1970).
2. See Daniel Lagache, *Les Hallucinations verbales et la parole* (Paris: Alcan, 1934).

it was admitted that all perception is only the retaining in consciousness of a sensorial stimulus, one found oneself obliged to presuppose an autostimulation of the central nervous system in the case of hallucination. From there we get the idea that hallucination is the revival of a weaker perception. On the other hand, according to this view, the knowledge of a language reduced itself to the arrangement of a certain number of engrams traced in the brain. Consciousness evoked the image of the word, and the word, by a process which is the inverse of that which one would suppose occurs in perception, disengaged the nervous influx which, at the level of the motor center, went on to give birth to the motor act, i.e., speech.

A whole neurology, even a whole psychology, came out of the initial ontological position. But since then the facts have proven that neither this neurology, nor this psychology, is valid.

A. *First Remark*

Once the patient is himself conscious of the difference between hallucination and perception, it becomes impossible to reduce one to the other and to explain hallucination as a simple excitation of the relevant nerve center. On the other hand, when an identity of nature between the two phenomena was hypothesized, it was impossible to penetrate the meaning of the pathological phenomenon. At the most, one could only have pity for those who perceived without having an exterior object for their perception. Indeed, there was nothing in hallucination that could be understood. In fact, there is so much to understand that even descriptions of the patient are already themselves interpretations.

B. *Second Remark*

Hallucination accompanies movements of the phonatory apparatus. These movements are either latent, roughly sketched out, or even visible. Hallucination, then, would be founded in speech itself.

It is thus a question of understanding the mechanism

according to which the subject grasps speech as something that comes from other people.

The originality of the phenomenon in comparison to "sensorial" phenomena will only appear after a confrontation with other problems. Following Lagache's analysis, we will compare true verbal hallucination with the following phenomena:

1. *Verbal obsession.* This is an obsession with a certain word which imposes itself upon the subject and forces the subject to use this word in an obsessive fashion even at the least appropriate times. The subject is forced to utter the word as one spits out a cherry pit to rid oneself of the annoying object.

In verbal hallucination we rediscover this character of the "in spite of itself." It constitutes the negative aspect of the illness. But it goes much further than this, since the speech will be attributed to other people.

2. *Complete motor verbal hallucination.* Accompanied by initial movements, it appears as a transition between the case in which the subject considers his words as coming from himself and that in which he considers them as coming from other people.

3. *Kinesthetic verbal hallucination.* Here, spoken words emanate neither from the subject nor from other people. The subject has the impression that he is submerged in a current of anonymous spoken words. For example, he hears bird calls as spoken words, and he hears them directly. It is not a question of a delirious interpretation.

4. *Motor verbal pseudo-hallucination.* In this case, there is no longer any localization in space. The subject has the impression that people are speaking to him through his brain. He has the impression that he is hearing "the language of thought." The sensorial phenomenon has completely disappeared. This is a question of a mental speech which is nothing else but accentuated interior language.

C. *Concluding Remarks*

This description has shown that *the central phenomenon is not the sensorial fact but rather the depersonalization.* The subject no longer has the impression that he coincides with his own speech. And this is the germ of the illusion of a speech that is foreign to him. For psychoanalysis, the relationships between the composite elements of the self (the *id* and the *superego*) are at once discordant relationships. The *superego* disavows the involuntary *id* element of the self and thus realizes a behavior of self-punishment. Meanwhile, if the tension created by the conflict is too strong, the subject will generally have a tendency to project onto other people this contemptible element of his self, thus bringing about a relaxation. The conflict between the self and other people is less wearisome than the conflict with oneself. For example, a child who has lied will accuse another child of a falsehood. A patient who has felt guilty about his mother's death will believe, several years later, that he himself is the object of a persecution.

Thus, the self and others are not two substances that are distinct from one another. Other people are what deliver me from my own *ambivalence:* we are both, he and I, two variables of the same system. By a mechanism of *pro*jection, I attribute to him qualities which in reality are my own, and inversely by *intro*jection I consider qualities which are his as my own.

D. *Application to Hallucination*

This is the same mechanism that we find in hallucination. At the same time that there is a passage from "I am an assassin" to "I have been assassinated," there is also passage from "I speak" to "I am spoken to." [3] To feel that one has been injured is to injure oneself.

Lagache has shown that all speech is a double action. When I listen to another speak, I am not silent; already I anticipate his spoken words, and I already have my answer, at least in outline form. Inversely, for the person who is speaking, there is an implicit belief in my comprehension. A "field of individually spoken

3. [This last "I am spoken to" is given in English following the French *je suis parlé*, which is related to *je parle* in the same way that there is movement from *je suis assassin* to *je suis assassiné*.]

words" establishes itself between us. The function of language is only a particular case of the general relation between self and others, which is the relation between two consciousnesses, of which each one projects itself *in the other.*

If one simply pushed this mechanism to an extreme, it would produce the hallucination. The hallucinator would be able to anticipate at what point in the reactions of his possible inter-locutors he would substitute himself totally for them and adopt a resolutely receptive attitude vis-à-vis his own spoken words.

The whole classical theory of hallucination has been built on the example of the *phantom limb.*[4] Now, the perception of the phantom limb has been reinterpreted; and the conclusions of the interpretation are absolutely incompatible with the classical conception of a perception provoked by the direct excitation of nerve centers. The patient had, for many months, lost the use of his fifth finger. After the amputation, he had the illusion of a phantom arm with a four-fingered hand. If the absence of feeling for a period of time is sufficient to block this illusion, it cannot be a question of an excitation of nerve centers. In this case, it is a question of a global phenomenon. The illusion is founded on a *corporal scheme* or body image (which is a scheme of all possible activities, rather than a scheme of the actual bodily state).

It is necessary to make a similar revision of hallucination in general. Speech must be considered as a total structure, a system by which one can attain communication with others. Hallucina-tion is not a relationship between subject and object; it is a rela-tionship of *being:* I exist through language in a relationship with others.

But is it legitimate to interpret the normal in light of the pathological? Certainly, this substantial identity between speak-ing [*parler*] and "being spoken" [*être parlé*] exists only for the patient; but if this confusion exists in the pathological state, it is because it already exists in an embryonic form in the normal person. In the normal person, there is already a germ of aliena-

---

4. [See Merleau-Ponty's *Phenomenology of Perception,* trans. Colin Smith (London: Routledge & Kegan Paul, 1962), for an elabo-rated discussion of this problem, which can be found principally in the section on the body.]

tion, a compelling relationship between the spoken and the heard.

Thus, we arrive at the following paradox: the normal subject would be the one who would not really consent to becoming himself except in contact with other people, who would recognize the enrichment that comes from discussion. The abnormal subject would be the one who would refuse this dialectic of the self. He would persist in considering language as only a kind of abstract logic. While nevertheless remaining conscious of this duality, he would feel restrained from placing one of the terms of the contradiction on an imaginary other.

[III] THE STUDY OF APHASIA

WILL IT NOT BE NECESSARY to revise these conclusions if we examine the physiological foundations of speech (localizations)?

How, in effect, can we conceive of language as being at the same time an intersubjective phenomenon and a purely individual one linked to the third left frontal convolution of the brain.

A. *Confronting of Two Theses*

In proportion to its development, the clinical analysis of aphasia (loss of speech, related to a disorder of the speech organs) has shown that the classical interpretations were false. The verbal image is not a brain trace: the central nervous system is not a *storehouse of images*. It is a center endowed with the organization of movements. It is only the locus of a function.

This is what confirms the following facts: the aphasiac is not someone who no longer speaks, but rather someone who speaks less or in another fashion. He remembers a word in one situation and not in another. For example, a patient is incapable of repeating the word "no," but when pushed further, he answers in exasperation: "no, I just cannot say that word." Thus, we arrive at the idea of a two-functioned language. There would be:

(1) *a concrete language,* whose role would be to respond to actual situations;

(2) *a categorial language,* which considers the word in itself as a purely abstract entity and which responds to fictitious situations or to "problems."

Aphasia would lead language back to its first function.

B. *Goldstein's Analysis of Language*

We reached the hypothesis that aphasia is an intellectual disorder in which the material aspects of language can in no way be attained. The patient would not have lost the automatic use of words as much as the disposition toward a certain type of language: the *categorial language.*

1. [*An example.*] Goldstein analyzed certain aphasiacs for whom the language disorder accompanied a more general disorder: the incapacity to class perceived objects. For example, one of them, when presented with a series of different colored skeins of wool and asked to classify them according to a fundamental color, was incapable of doing so. He did not know how to assemble the different shades of the same color. He proceeded in a much more detailed fashion, placing the samples side by side so as to compare them. He did not follow any directive principle and, in the course of the experiment, he suddenly tried to group the different samples according to another principle, for example, according to their degree of saturation or brightness.

2. *Interpretation.* The normal subject is capable of considering a concrete object as representing one category. His behavior is categorial. If the patient appears to change his principle, it is because, in reality, *there is none.* He has only a concrete experience of suitability or of unsuitability.

The patient can, however, recognize the color when he is in the presence of an object characterized by this color, for example, cherry-red or bottle-green. The possibility of rediscovering the name of the color can be explained indirectly: the consciousness which envisions "red" is an abstraction, a disinterested attitude of pure investigation, while the consciousness that envisions the cherry is concrete. It is through the concrete consciousness of the cherry that the patient rediscovers the abstract name: red.

What is of interest in Goldstein's research is that it reveals the role of a *replacement function* which, for the outside observer, masks the problem. The subject answers: "it is blue," while at the same time thinking "pastel blue."

There are subjects who no longer possess the notion of number and who, nevertheless, by a function of replacement, can give the appearance of counting. They make each object correspond to a finger and each finger correspond to a number in the automatic recitation of a series.

This discovery invites the psychiatrist to a much deeper examination, while before it was, above all, a question of determining the functions that the patient was capable of performing and those that he could no longer perform. Now, it is a question of investigating, even in the cases where the patient succeeds, *by what path,* or *in what sense,* he succeeds. The "exterior verbal knowledge" which is only an appearance of knowledge can mask major deficiencies in true naming.[5]

But what is the exact significance of Goldstein's analysis? Apparently, it is in the meaning of Pierre Marie's work distinguishing the case of anarthria from the case of *true aphasia.*[6] It seems that language is conditioned by thought. Whereas Broca considered language as the summation of cerebral traces, it is a global phenomenon and seems to require the general functioning of thought.[7] Thus, there seems to be a reversal of the initial positions. Contrary to Broca's position, Goldstein presents an idealist conception, which shows a power of thought behind the linguistic

5. See Adhémar Gelb and Kurt Goldstein, "Uber Farbennamenamnesie," *Psychologische Forschung,* 1925; and W. Hochheimer, "Analyse eines Seelenblinden von der Sprache aus," *Psychologische Forschung,* 1932.

6. [Anarthria: congenital disability for the acquisition of motor speech skills. See, for example, Pierre Marie, *Travaux et mémoires* (Paris: Masson, 1926), Vol. I: *L'Aphasie.*]

7. [See Paul Broca, *Des Anévrysmes et leur traitement* (Paris: Labé, 1856).]

function. Starting with the exterior, he returns to the interior, to pure consciousness, to a spiritual function that could not involve sentences or nouns: an indivisible "symbolic function."

But, then, in what way is it vulnerable? In reality, neither Broca's attitude nor the idealist nor intellectualist attitude takes the linguistic phenomenon into account. For one, there is no speaking subject; there are only verbal images. For the other, there is no speaking subject; there is simply a thinking subject. The theory of aphasia must pass beyond this second position as well as the first, and it must determine the respective roles of *corporal conditioning* on the one hand and of *intellectual consciousness* on the other. Now, when one carefully examines Goldstein's analyses, one sees that, in their best moments, they are not oriented toward intellectualism.

3. *The physiological facts.* No serious author has rejected the notion of cerebral localizations, but it is no longer a question of the relationship between containing and the contained. Goldstein has proposed that there are two truths to be remembered: the whole brain contributes to every partial operation, and hence there is no mosaic functioning.

This does not mean that the functions of the brain are diffused. All the parts of the brain do not contribute to each operation in the same way. One plays the role of *figure* and the other the role of *ground*. There is a localization in the sense that the integrity of a certain part of the brain is absolutely necessary for the proper working of a certain function. The substituted function is never the exact equivalent of the destroyed function.

For example, in the perception of a figure against a ground, the occipital region plays the essential role, but the whole brain comes into play.

4. *The clinical facts.* Goldstein never supposed that the categorial function was absolute spiritually. The patient's inability to classify is linked to a transformation of his *own perception*. Whereas the normal subject is capable of immediate organization of his perceptual field according to the lines of force, there is, on the contrary, a dispersal of this field in the patient. The failure of the categorial attitude is, or implies, a change in the structuring of perception. Behind the act of designation, there is no dis-

tinct intellectual operation: the categorial function is incarnated in the word, giving it its physiognomy. When it fails, one has the impression that the word has been "emptied," that it has lost "what rendered it appropriate for the act of designation" (Goldstein).

It now remains for us to understand how thought inhabits language, how the meaning inhabits the word.[8] Thought supports linguistic material at every level. This phenomenon is apparent in the patient whose syntactic thought develops at the expense of the articulatory physiognomy, showing that thought conditions the two phenomena. The language of the aphasiac has lost an essential quality: it has ceased to be alive. It is in this way that one of Goldstein's patients could only speak when he was following a plan without any personal accent or improvisation. There was something colorless about the totality of his language, a total absence of style.

We must place the accent on the *productivity of language:* language is a totality of instruments for our relationships with people. It reflects to what degree we are capable of inventions. It is a manifestation of the link that we have with other people and with ourselves (Goldstein).

In a book that appeared last year, Goldstein clarifies his ideas further.[9] He redefines the categorial attitude and then introduces a new notion: that of "instrumentalities of speech." [10] He shows that these two functions closely depend on one another, that the loss of one is harmful to the other.

What is interesting about the analysis is that it does not attain the classical separation between the corporeal and the spiritual. This is the same problem that we note at the level of the categorial attitude and at the level of instrumentalities of speech. It is a question not of reducing language to thought but

8. See the special issue of the *Journal de psychologie*, 1933: Kurt Goldstein, "L'Analyse de l'aphasie et l'essence du langage." [This article has been reproduced in *Essais sur le langage* ed. Jean-Claude Pariente (Paris: Les Editions de Minuit, 1969), pp. 259–330.]

9. Kurt Goldstein, *Language and Language Disturbances* (New York: Grune & Stratton, 1948).

10. [In English in the text.]

of introducing thought into language, and it follows that this insertion will be more or less satisfying, that language will appear as normal or abnormal. We will first study the categorial attitude and second the instrumentalities of speech, trying to bring to light the osmosis of the two functions and the role of thought in each one of them.

C. *The Categorial Attitude*

This attitude renders a series of operations possible. The principles of these operations are:

(1) the capacity to take on a mental task, to take the initiative, to execute a linguistic performance upon request;

(2) the possibility of examining the same problem under different aspects;

(3) the capacity to consider and to react to two independent stimuli simultaneously;

(4) the capacity to separate the essential from the accidental;

(5) the capacity to conceive of a future, that is, to think the possible as well as the real;

(6) the capacity to distinguish the *ego* from the external world.

When there is a destruction of the categorial function, one notes some disorders at the instrumental level, for example, a patient who cannot make use of a multiplication table, even when he knows it by heart.

It is easy to differentiate the cases where the instrumental function is attained directly and those where it is only indirectly attained through the categorial attitude.

In the latter case, one notes:

(1) that the linguistic apparatus functions at certain moments and not at others;

(2) that words have become individual words, with concrete significations which no longer have any relationship with their context.

For example, the word "thing," which for the normal person covers a notion, becomes for the patient a manner of designating an object for which he no longer knows the name, a means of masking the deficiency.

But the categorial function is incarnated in the object. Its relationship to language is the external relationship of cause to effect. The word is a body through which an intention appears. Speech is not a simple automatism in the service of thought. It is the instrument of actualization of thought. Thought is truly realized only when it has found its verbal expression.

For the patient, on the contrary, the word appears as a sonorous complex. It is no longer the vehicle of thought. It lives in an external relationship with thought.

D. *Instrumentalities of Speech*

The disorders that result from the loss of the instrumentalities of speech are very different:

(1) there is a confusion of letters or words;

(2) instead of the word that he is seeking, the subject uses one with the same physiognomy (the same number of letters and syllables);

(3) there is a lack of little words (prepositions, adverbs, articles);

(4) there are problems of repetition.

The words are worn, but they have retained their significative power. It is in this way that we see thought incarnated in instrumental language. By what mechanism? This is what Goldstein will try to show by borrowing from Humboldt's notion of *innere Sprachform*.

For Humboldt, the *innere Sprachform* is completely different from the notion of certain psychologists with regard to interior language (a simple evocation of a certain number of verbal images).[11] This is the reflection in language of the world view [*perspective sur le monde*] appropriate to a given culture. Each language has its own way of expressing different relationships,

11. [See Wilhelm von Humboldt, *Linguistic Variability and Intellectual Development,* trans. George C. Buck and Frithjof A. Raven (Coral Gables, Fla.: University of Miami Press, 1971).]

like time and space. For example, the structure of Greek will indicate an "architechtonic of time" appropriate to the Greeks. Even the manner of distributing the accents, the flections, and even the use of the article are expressive of a world view [*une vue du monde*].

The *innere Sprachform* is the totality of processes and expressions that are produced when we are at the point of expressing our thought or of understanding the thought of other people.

The juncture of pure thought and of language occurs, then, in the *innere Sprachform*, which is differentiated according to the manner in which we speak or write, according to the manner in which we address ourselves or others. A layer of significations interposes itself between language (the totality of words) and thought. These significations presuppose a certain relationship with the language. It is this kind of nonexplicit thought in language that constitutes *style*.

We can now complete what we said at the beginning of this course concerning the acquisition of phonemes. Whereas for Jakobson this acquisition is determined by objective laws, for Goldstein, on the contrary, the phonematic development occurs according to a certain phonematic "style" which is not, in itself and at the outset, prescribed by any necessity. Just as an organism, far from realizing all the movements of which its structure renders it capable, adopts among all its defined postures privileged ones that conform to a fundamental organization of his behavior—to an *Urbild* of the individual under consideration (for example, the attitude of repose of an individual cannot be explained by his anatomy)—so is the systematic form of phonemes used by a linguistic community elaborated by that linguistic community as the best means of expressing its world view.

Let us now reexamine what Piaget has said about children's language from the same point of view. Words are not simple indicators of language, as he claims. From the beginning of language they legitimately have what Goldstein calls a "situational value." The child uses certain words before he fully understands their signification, in the way that the adult, when learning a foreign language, uses certain locutions of which he does not know the meaning but which he knows how to apply in the appropriate situation. It is this language that does not take itself into account which Piaget calls egocentric. For Goldstein, it is the means by which a child can have access to language and by which an adult can continue to maintain its reality.

Other facts reinforce his thesis:

1. In repetition, the customary process is not to repeat the sentence as it is presented to the ear, but rather to understand it first and then to give it an equivalent personal reproduction. This is to show to what extent thought shines through signs to give their meanings, to what extent language least masks thought. Paying attention to language per se is difficult. This is because language is *pregnant* with meaning, which, in the end, is only possible through its *innere Sprachform*.

2. In talkative people, the abundance of speech develops to the detriment of signification. In the pathological condition, this same phenomenon appears in the patient who has lost the use of his interior language. He *talks* more in order to *say* less. The *innere Sprachform* is this expressive life of language which renders it capable of *style*.

All language is mind. It is a verbal melody which presupposes an intellectual vigilance. But the mind that governs language is not mind for itself; it is paradoxically a mind that possesses itself only by losing itself in language.

E. *Conclusion*

Broca's theory has been surpassed, without the modern analysis of aphasia being a return to idealism. The meaning that inhabits language is the situational meaning of which we have already spoken. It is easy to define when it is applied to concrete things and more difficult when it is applied to more abstract words like "understanding" or "philosophy." Nevertheless, these concepts can also be considered as elements of a cultural situation.

The *innere Sprachform* is a mental landscape common to all the members of a linguistic community. It is that which makes it possible for some people to coexist with others through a cultural milieu.

3 / The Contribution of Linguistics

[I] [INTRODUCTION]

TODAY LINGUISTS NO LONGER RAISE the issue of the origin of language. There are many reasons for this:

1. The origin of language considers the prehistory of language and not its history. There are no investigations based on written traces. Hence there is no positive solution. However, the objection is not decisive.

Jespersen sees a positive means of approaching this problem.[1] One might start with the present state of language and then establish a graph of evolution that can be extended back inductively to the origin of language.

2. To explain the origin of language is to try to derive it from other things. Now, there is always a gap between the forms of natural expression and language as such.

Attempts to fill in this gap were made at the end of the nineteenth century:

(a) Some people tried to show that articulated language is a variety of a simpler language founded on imitation. In this case, the relationship between sign and signification is founded on *onomatopoeia*, representing the initial form of all words. For ex-

1. [Jens Otto Harry Jespersen, *Language: Its Nature, Development and Origin* (London: Allen & Unwin, 1922).]

ample, the song of the rooster, "cock-a-doodle-doo," has yielded the word "cock" and a whole family of words: "coquette," "cocky," "cockade" . . .

No one supports this idea any longer. Onomatopoeia is the equivalent of an ideogram in writing. But the ideogram is not stable. It gradually fills itself up with a certain meaning as it becomes syllabic or alphabetic writing. Similarly, language cannot be traced back to such narrow modes of signification.

(b) Another attempt has been to link up words with *emotional manifestations*, for example, exclamations. But on the one hand, exclamations intervene in order to say something when one is surprised, and on the other hand, they vary from one language to another. Hence, they have an institutional value.

The derivation of language from *the cry* applies only to a very small number of interjections.

The expression of articulated language rests on a different principle from that which renders the imitated word possible. That which makes the word "sun" designate the sun is not the resemblance between the word and the thing, nor is it the internal character of either. Rather, it is the relationship between the word "sun" and the totality of all English words; it is the manner in which it differentiates itself from them. The word only has meaning through the whole *institution* of language.

Many linguists think, therefore, that to pose the problem of the origin of language would be to reduce it to modes of expression that have nothing in common with it. They want to concern themselves only with constituted language.

However, at the very least one cannot deny the historicity of language. We participate in partial creations, whatever their origins may be, in terms of nonlinguistic modes of expression. These creations are *conditioned*. One must admit that there are *thresholds*, that one does not arrive at just anything starting with just anything. One must admit that, in certain constellations, a given creation which was not possible before becomes possible now. To admit a history of language is not simply to arrive at a certain state without passing through successive levels.

There is a *causal conception* of history which postulates that there is more, or as much, in the cause as in the effect. And there is a conception of history which is a simple explanation of what was originally given. These two conceptions deny the role of time. Language does not accommodate itself either to one or to the other. It obliges us to consider history as a contingent course and as a logic of things, where phenomena can sketch themselves out and then be systematized by acts of social life or of thought. For example, the negation *pas* in French started out being a word which designated the progression of a man walking (*je ne fais pas,* meaning: "I do not advance a step"). It is by a slipping [*glissement*] that the word *pas* took on its negative meaning. Thanks to an equivocal moment, there was renewal and acquisition. After a certain period of use, the word became a new instrumentality of speech. At every moment of time, language is renewed from the past and modified by a series of escapes. Thus we have to admit, if not a birth of language, at least a movement of language toward the more expressive forms from less expressive ones. These forms would have to be sufficiently different from our present language to merit the name of a *prelanguage.*

It is forms of this type that Jespersen tries to reconstitute. He notes the progressive elimination of sounds which are considered as the longest and most difficult. Primitive words ought to have the same relationship to our own words as the plesiosaurus has to animals of today.

Our language is less emotional than its rudimentary forms. There would not have been an initial difference between the act of speaking and the act of singing.

Ancient grammars have a more synthetic form; the modern ones have a more analytic form (e.g., Latin is more synthetic than French). Verbs could have varied according to a great number of aspects: gender, direct or indirect object, etc., . . . Archaic speech would have been much less complicated than modern speech.

The initial form of language, therefore, would have been a kind of song. Men would have sung their feelings before communicating their thought. Just as writing was at first painting, language at first would have been song, which, if it analyzed itself, would have become a linguistic sign. It is through the exercise of this song that men would have tried out their power of expression.

One seeks, then, to describe certain forms of prelinguistic expression which, without being the *causes* of language, would be its *cradle*. In a similar fashion, Révész, in his mediocre book entitled *The Origins and Prehistory of Language*, describes some experiments of contact and of calling which furnish language, if not with conditions of possibility, at least with certain conditions of realization.[2]

One cannot speak of an empirical origin of language. One can at the very least describe prelinguistic forms starting with those which *a man has the tendency* to speak. At that point language becomes imminent.

Even for those authors who admit to an evolution, the appearance of articulated language is like an *Ursprung* (a springing forth). Linguists invite us, then, to place ourselves inside language and not to consider it from the outside.

We could be interested either in their general philosophical conclusions or in their scientific studies. If we adopt the second point of view, we collide with objections that are lodged against the philosopher who uses a positivist discipline. One reproaches him for: (*a*) linking the fate of philosophy to the scientific system in question (that is, to relative and provisional theories), *sacrificing philosophy to science;* (*b*) reinterpreting scientific phenomena, thus giving them a signification that they do not have, that is, *sacrificing science to philosophy.*

These two objections imply the necessity to choose between science and philosophy. Science is a construction elaborated by men, destined to elucidate, by means of rigorous methods, a certain number of their own or other people's experiences. Whether or not we can expect a knowledge of being from science, no philosophy can dispense with finding a philosophical link and status for its methods of "verification." Since linguistics is the most rigorous existing examination of language as an institution, one cannot conceive of a philosophy of language which is not obliged to collect and articulate on the basis of its own truths those truths that the linguist has established. If one considers philosophy as

2. [Géza Révész, *The Origins and Prehistory of Language*, trans. J. Butler (New York: Philosophical Library, 1956).]

the elucidation of human experience, and science as an essential moment in this experience, the dilemma disappears.

We will not ask linguists for their philosophical conclusions (as philosophers, their thinking is no more solid than others). We will seek to participate in their experience of language.

The linguist, by comparing one language to another, makes each one appear according to a structure [*sur un fond*] which suddenly unveils the language to those who spoke it but who did not *see* it. The comparative and objective study is indispensable for opening our eyes to this language that we think we understand because we speak it.

In principle, linguistics studies language objectively: that is, it considers language as it is, "behind the backs" (Hegel) of subjects who speak. But, in fact, as we shall see, the objective method converges with a direct reflection on language.

[II]   [THE STUDY OF LINGUISTICS]

A. *Sounds*

THE STUDY OF CHANGES in the phonemic system which intervene in the course of the history of a language is *phonetics*. Do sounds depend solely on our phonatory organs? If such were the case, one could expect there to be laws of universal vectors [*vections*] according to which languages tend to transform themselves in a certain direction. Now, according to common consent, phonetic laws are only valid within a given historical period. This allows us to presume that these laws are not comparable to physical laws, or, more precisely, that they are never guided by an unconditioned necessity. There would have been a dependence of the law vis-à-vis a certain historical structure of language. In the same way, a physical law, for example, the rate of falling bodies, is valid only in a certain state of the world. The law of falling bodies is understandable only in a system in which the speed of rotation of the earth does not go beyond a certain limit. The whole law is consistent with a certain coefficient of fact (Brunschvicg). This is even truer for linguistics, where laws are affected by a coefficient of facility. Thus, they do not allow for any predicting and are only certain when it is a question of the past (Vendryes).

On the other hand, the phonetic phenomenon does not constitute an order in itself which would leave out the speaking subject. Even in terms of sounds, we see phonemes from other languages appearing at certain moments. Internal to language, they are determined not by phonetic necessity, but by phenomena such as imitation. A logical element is reintroduced as an afterthought by putting the language into practice. We note, for example, the effects of hyperurbanism or hyperdialectism, which are voluntary overemphases on the part of city dwellers and country folk arising from a need to distinguish themselves.

Finally, we must account for the extent to which sounds that we use in language are richer than those emitted naturally by our phonatory apparatus. One never equals the richness and variety of sounds in a language by pronouncing *just any sound*. Thus, beneath these three relationships, it is clear that the sonorous phenomenon in language is already of a transnatural order.

B. *Grammar*

The grammarians of the seventeenth and eighteenth centuries, being inspired by grammatical categories that are not adapted to the real structure of French, give us a deformed image rather than knowledge.

Etymology can also give a false idea of a word. In effect, when the meaning of a word is not behind but in front, this prospective meaning is not necessarily the result of past meanings. "We are not the sons of our ancestors; rather, we choose our ancestors" (Aron).[3] This could apply to popular etymology, that is, the choice by which man expresses the effective meaning which he actually gives to a word.

Semantemes are words like "sky," "table," etc., while *mor-*

3. [See, for example, Raymond Aron, *Introduction to the Philosophy of History,* trans. George J. Irwin (Boston: Beacon, 1961).]

phemes express the relationships between words: "to," "of," "for" . . .

Morphology is the study of the totality of forms which reunite words. The notion of morpheme is very generalized, and linguists have shown that the absence of the sign is a sign (a "zero-morpheme"). For example, the nominative, which requires no word ending in a given language, is designated by this absence of inflection, in the same way that there are expressive silences in music. In addition to the inventory of manifest morphemes, the complete morphology would therefore have to decipher these latent morphemes. Here are some examples:

1. There are some languages (Fula) in which negation is marked by *intonation.*[4]

2. The expression "he has done" is composed of three words: linguists have asked whether or not this analysis is conventional. They compare an expression of this type to characteristic morphemes of the aorist in Greek.[5] For the man who speaks English, the expression "he has done" is not composed of a pronoun, a verb, and a participle. It is the total expression in which "he" is equivalent to the "σ" and to the augment [6] in the Greek aorist.

3. In Chinese, the relationship of dependence between principle words is marked by *the order of words*. There are no positive morphemes; nevertheless, the Chinese express morphological relations just as strongly as we do, through particularities designated for that purpose.

4. In French, when one says *Pierre frappe Paul,* the only morpheme that is expressed is the *e* in *frappe*.

5. This analysis of the notion of morpheme leads us to generalize considerably: the morpheme is far from being a word to which a positive concept can be made to correspond.

4. [*Peul,* or *Peulh* in French, a West African language.]
5. [Aorist: a verb-tense, expressing an action, usually past, where the time is indefinite or unimportant (Greek *epempsa,* "I sent" vs. *pepompha,* "I have sent"). From Mario Pei, *Glossary of Linguistic Terminology* (New York: Anchor, 1966).]
6. [Augment: a prefixed element (vowel, diphthong, or vowel-lengthening) used in Classical Greek (imperfect *epempon* from *pempō; ērchon* from *archō*). From Pei, *Glossary of Linguistic Terminology.*]

There has sometimes been a derivation of the morpheme from the semanteme. For example, *casa* in Latin becomes *chez* in French. The semanteme is emptied of its meaning, by which process there emerged a meaning which at times remained imprecise. It is appropriate of the morpheme to be a grammatical tool, characterized by *values of usage* rather than by *significations*. In certain cases, the morpheme appears to us as extraordinarily undefinable. It is impossible to give a *definition* to the preposition *à* in French, to which eight possible translations correspond in German (*zu, nach, an, in, mit, auf, bei, um*). This remark will be useful to us when we ask, along with Saussure, how language signifies.

We have seen that the apparently simple distinction between semanteme and morpheme becomes confused the minute we consider it at close range. Thus the *personal pronouns*, which were semantemes at the beginning, have ended up by becoming purely and simply morphemes. For example in the French *je le dis*, the pronoun attaches itself to the verb more and more closely. The conjugation *je dis, tu dis, il dis* (pronounced *jedi, tudi, idi*) is equivalent to the Latin *dico, dicis, dicit*. *Jedi, tudi, idi* can be considered as the extension of a previous flection of the word.

It is impossible to fix words to an absolutely definitive grammatical function, for, in reality, there are no concepts of noun, pronoun, etc. The word is like a *tool defined by a certain usage* even though we are unable to give an exact conceptual formula to this usage. (This remark is valid for most grammatical categories.)

The *gender*, even if it appeared to be founded originally on observable or mystical characteristics of the object, no longer has any intrinsic signification today.

Each time that a French word is not accompanied by an article, which renders the gender quite apparent, the gender of the word tends to become ambiguous. For example, French words beginning with a vowel (like *l'aurore, l'abîme*) have a tendency to change gender because they do not have an article which maintains their original gender. The gender tends to be a simple indicator which differentiates words, a "classifier."

The *number* corresponds to a certain aspect of things. But it is far from delineating the relationship between things and far from deriving an absolutely univocal signification. Should one write *confiture de groseille* or *confiture de groseilles*? [7] This hesitation is the consequence of the fact that the French plural covers two indistinct significations: *plurality* and *collectivity*.

The same remark is valid for most linguistic categories that always conceal beyond their principal meaning a latent meaning in the process of development or regression. There is not just one system of categories that is immutable and inherent in things. Categories evolve: for example, the French plural *bourgeonne* (a collective term). Language contains some significations that are acquired or available and others that are in the process of suggesting themselves. One would impoverish the language by reducing it to just what is actually stated.

In the case of *tenses*, the distinction between present, past, and future appears to be founded in things. But there are languages which have no future and others which possess tenses other than these—that is, which understand time differently.

It is impossible to understand the conjugations of Greek or of Indo-European if one does not introduce the *aspect* of time, which distinguishes the action envisioned in an instant. The aspect would be a category of *duration* rather than a category of time.

Thus, there is no objective evidence of grammatical time, but simply different *linguistic instruments* for exploring time. In Hebrew, the future serves as both future and past in narrative, while the preterit can serve as future. We say that there is an indecision because we try to think the mode of the articulation of time in terms of our own formulations. In reality, if we succeed in thinking this conjugation according to its "own architechtonic" (G. Guillaume), we will see that it maintains its meaning and allows for a communication of the fundamental relationships of time. Moreover, one sees this aspect emerging in French, influenced by the need to express oneself. Words constructed with a *re-* replace the simple form when one envisions only the *result* and not the process. Whereas initially *re-* implied the idea of

7. [*Confiture de groseille:* gooseberry jam; *confiture de groseilles:* jam of gooseberries. The problem does not seem to exist in English.]

reiteration, later it took on a different signification and indicated a nuance of aspect for which French has no official designation. For example, *abattre* and *rabattre*, *abaisser* and *rabaisser*. Therefore, we see in a given language the equivalent of what can be found in another, expressed with more or less technical skill. If there is a unity of languages across languages, we must find it in a common effort toward expansion and not in a system of "universal" categories. It is a unity in the order of existence and not in the order of essence.

French conjugation contains enough exceptions to its own rules for one to consider it a linguistic tool rather than a representation of time.

Active and passive. The theoretical distinction between these two grammatical categories includes the fact that one performs an action and the other undergoes it. For example, "the cat eats the mouse" is active, while "the mouse is eaten by the cat" is passive. But the passive form is not confined to this latter usage. Moreover, one performs no action when he says: "I am dying" or "I am suffering." Within the active conjugation, there are passive forms, such as "I am done." [8]

Certain languages have only the passive mode. The expressive apparatus cannot be considered as the summation of signs for discrete and juxtaposed significations. It must content itself with an evocation of pure understanding.

Transitive and intransitive. In principle, one admits a direct object and the other does not. In reality, there is no rigorously defined conceptual value to this instrumentality of speech, nor is there a logico-grammatical parallelism. *Noces tibi* [you are hurting yourself] has a transitive meaning. Thus, the possibility of a universal grammar remains problematic, since language is made up of significations in the state of being born. This is the case because language is in movement and is not fixed; and perhaps because one must recognize in the last analysis that there are "flowing significations," as Husserl has noted in his later writings.

All of our distinctions between kinds of words (pronouns, ad-

8. [Merleau-Ponty gives *je suis allé* as his example.]

jectives, verbs) are schematic in relation to the usage of the language.

However, there does exist an irreducible difference between two kinds of sentences: (*a*) *the verbal sentence,* which contains a verb other than the verb "to be"; (*b*) *the nominal sentence,* which contains the verb "to be" and expresses the properties of an object.

But the Aristotelian analysis is insufficient not only, as we have often stated, for passing from language to thought, *but also for characterizing language itself.* Linguists refuse to reduce the verbal sentence to the nominal one.

Finally, other distinctions of meaning are expressed by *style* and not by grammar. *The order of words,* in certain languages without morphemes, determines the meaning. In other languages, the order of words is relatively optional, thus leaving the field open for nuances of style. In Latin, *homo est avarus* means: it happens to be the case that this man is avaricious, while *avarus homo est* means: avarice is the [characteristic] fault of this man.

This is particularly apparent when one compares written language to spoken language. The following sentence in written language: "As for me, I do not have the time to think about this matter" becomes in spoken language: "When would I have the time to think about things like that?" (Vendryes)

According to certain people, it is out of spoken language, hence out of *living communication,* that grammar draws its origins. In that case, there is a *pre-grammar* which produces the grammar by stabilizing itself.

After considering the stabilized morphology, it will be necessary to study *changing morphology.* Language is characterized by two contradictory needs: *a need for uniformity* and *a need for expressivity.* It is necessary that a form be used to be understood, and yet a form that is used too frequently loses its meaning—for example, "terrific," "unbelievable" [*"formidable," "épatant"*]. The need for expressivity fights against the wearing out of words and forms; it even arouses linguistic creations at certain moments.

Naturally, these creations do not follow any preestablished plan. They are systematic, but for the most part they depend upon chance in the history of language. For example, the Italian accent on the next to last syllable of words has weakened the last syllable; but at the same time it has necessitated a new system of nonflectional expression. French, which emerged from the Latin, began "repairing," by luck, damaged flections. For example, the participles *vu* ["seen"], *tenu* ["held"], *rompu* ["broken"] have been incorporated into the French by analogy with words from Vulgar Latin ending with -*utus*. But that did not suffice. It was as though a new system of expression allowed itself to appear: articles and pronouns were developed, the need for prepositions transformed full words into prepositions, for example, *chez* (from *casa*) ["at the house of"], *excepté* ["except"], *malgré* ["in spite of"], *sauf* ["with the exception of"], *plein* (*plein les yeux*) ["full of"].

The erosion and decadence of an expressive system left behind it some debris that has been regrasped, reworked, and rescued, as if by a new wave of expressions. The erosion of the last syllable in Latin, which resulted in an accentuation on the penultimate, suddenly *became* the positive fact that in French there is an accent on the last syllable. Everything occurs in language as if the mind [*esprit*] were constantly taking chances. Therefore, it is a question of a kind of blind mind [*esprit*] whose nature we will have to render more precise.

C. *Vocabulary (Semantics)*

Although linguists do not, without reservations, claim that a word can have an identity through time (we have already seen that etymology does not give the real meaning), they are nevertheless obliged to admit that *absolutus* has rendered *absolu* in French [and "absolute" in English], for example. If this were not the case, comparative morphology and even phonetics would be impossible. But this identity through time is "blurred," like certain "snapshots" in photography. Words that are indistinguishable in living language, for example *louer* (meaning "to rent an apartment") and *louer* (meaning "to praise"), are different for etymologists because they come from two different words, *locare* and *laudare*. Etymologists consider some words to be identical, admitting only that they have *several meanings;* while, in reality, considered in the present state of language, these meanings are no longer related. Thus, we find three meanings of the verb *rapporter:* One can speak of a plot of land which yields [*rapporte*] a good income, a dog which retrieves [*rapporte*] the stick, and a child who tells [*rapporte*] a tale. *Maréchal (ferrant)* ["blacksmith"] and *Maréchal (de France)* ["Marshal of France"] have the same etymology but no relation in meaning. Similarly, when I speak of a *plume* for writing, I am not thinking of a bird feather [*plume* in French], although that is nevertheless the origin of the writing *plume.* The polysemy [9] of words is such that, in a given sentence, one can say that the word put back into its context, not the word itself, has a univocal meaning. But the context itself is constituted by other words, which also have many meanings. Thus, an interaction between words is produced which ends up by attributing to *each one* the meaning which is compatible with the others. In turn, one attributes to these others the meaning compatible with that of the first. A problem of the same order occurs in perception. Here each element of the perceptual field receives the chromatic, spatial, and significative value which is assigned to it by a whole *which, by hypothesis, we cannot yet use.* We can finally understand the constitution of such a *Gestalt* in the perceived world only if we refer to our bodily powers and organs as that which in us, are capable of realizing such an interplay of parts with the whole. We must guess by their familiarity with the perceived world what the configuration of the whole world will be, and we must confer upon each detail its appropriate value. Likewise, in living language and in contemporary communication, we will never understand how a sentence can present us with an immediate meaning, giving us the very presence of the thought of others, if we, as the subject who understands, are pure understanding. We will never understand this if we, as subject, are limited to an inventory of all the possible significations of each of the words and those of the whole. We will never understand this if we consider that the subject is a *thinking subject* rather than a *speaking subject.* Language

9. [In the text we find *polyrésie,* but this is surely *polysémie.*]

functions with respect to thought as the body does with respect to perception.

To complete our discussion of semantic vocabulary, it is impossible to delimit the words of a language, to make a complete inventory. Certain words arise in us only when we need them, in the same way that the spark is not contained in the stone but is formed by the contact with the metal that strikes it. Language, as an instrument, is not comparable to a hammer which has a finite number of uses. It is rather like a piano out of which one can draw an indefinite number of melodies. In an inventory of vocabulary, will we count a word each time there is a signification? Will we count as part of an individual's vocabulary words for which he does not know the exact meaning even though he uses them appropriately? (Most French people do not know what a linnet [10] is, except through the expression: *tête de linotte,* which means a "harebrained person" or a "scatterbrain.") Will we count, as part of contemporary French, the words "1900," [11] which are still basically understood, but which are tending to disappear? To claim that one can count the words of a language is to suppose that this language is formed by a finite number of signs and significations, while it is really a system of unified expressions whose applications are not always *countable.*

In truth, a language is not made up of *words,* each of which is endowed with one or several meanings. Each word has its meaning only inasmuch as it is sustained in this signification by all the others. The same holds true for these others. The only reality is the *Gestalt* of language. In order for a word to endure in its meaning, it is necessary that it be supported by others. *Captivus* (and its derivative *captif*), supported by *capio,* retains its meaning without changing. However, *chétif,* which means "puny" or "pitiful," slips into another meaning. The possession

10. [Linnet: "A common small finch of the Old World, with plumage varyingly grey, red, pied, or nearly white."—Webster.]

11. [Though he uses the numerals "1900," Merleau-Ponty must be referring here to the articulated expression *"dix-neuf cent,"* as opposed to the more contemporary *"mille neuf cent."* This is perhaps analogous to the relative infrequency of the expression "nineteen hundred and seventy-three" as compared to "nineteen seventy-three."]

of meaning by the word is possible only in a very fragile situation of equilibrium. A word retains its meaning only when it is frequently used in different contexts. (The word *frustre,* which originally applied solely to a kind of money in which the effigy was erased, changed its meaning and now signifies "rough," because the checks and balances of varied contexts did not serve to maintain its initial meaning.) But if the word is employed too often and in too many contexts, it ends up by being attracted to each of them, and thus changes its meaning.

D. [*Conclusions*]

The unity which relates all the phenomena that we have encountered within these three sections (on phonetics, morphology, and vocabulary) also exists between these three orders of phenomena. It is the combined and counterbalanced action of phonetics, morphology, and vocabulary that is the life of a language. But, in a sense, the same unity maintains itself gradually across the development of different languages. We arrive finally, with Vendryes, at the idea of a unity of language-function across languages. By this, he is not dreaming of a universal grammar which would dominate all empirical grammars according to its conceptual system. Vendryes wants to speak of a concrete universality which realizes itself only gradually and finds itself treating the expressive desire which animates languages rather than the transitory forms which are its result.

"A language is an ideal which can be sought, but never found; a potential reality never actually realized; a becoming which never comes." [12] Language is an entity, comparable to the Kantian idea, resulting from the totalization in an infinity of all the convergent means of expression. French defines itself in the instant as the common aim of all subjects who speak it to the extent that they are able to communicate among themselves.

The success of this communication does not prohibit

12. [See Joseph Vendryes, *Language: A Linguistic Introduction to History,* trans. Paul Radin (New York: Barnes & Noble, 1951), p. 243.]

quantitative differences from transforming themselves into qualitative differences in an imperceptible progression from generation to generation. French is not an objective reality which can be sliced up along strict boundaries in space and time; it is a dynamic reality, a *Gestalt* in the simultaneous and the successive. It is a whole which culminates in certain distinctive properties, but which has no precise point of beginning and end. We cannot give an exact date to the appearance of French, although, at the end of a certain time of evolution, we may note a certain "architechtonic" (G. Guillaume) which is no longer that of Latin. It inevitably overflows its "limits," since it is never a single figure separating itself from a ground. Even a common language like French can acquire an imputed unity by nonlinguistic (political) factors. But dialects which are abandoned to spontaneous linguistic forces never achieve a unity. The isogloss [13] lines are not superimposable; in this case, we can say that French is like Provençal.

[III] [PHILOSOPHICAL IMPLICATIONS]

FROM THIS CONTACT with some linguistic facts, the philosopher can already extract several pieces of information.

A. *Phonemes and Grammar*

1. Concerning phonemes, we have seen that when one of them is dropped in a language, the language undergoes a systematic change (all the words in which it appeared lose it), even though there was no common decision. This occurrence is analogous to the loss of certain elements of the "corporeal schema" which one observes in certain illnesses. It has been noted that many patients are not aware of their sensory or motor deficiencies; [14] one is led to explain this fact by noting that the

13. Isogloss: a line separating areas called isogloss areas, where the language differs with respect to a given feature or features, a line marking the boundaries within which a given phenomenal feature is to be found. From Pei, *Glossary of Linguistic Terminology*.
14. The Ganser syndrome.

subject avoids any task which would necessitate the intervention of the affected member or organ. This member or organ is placed "out of circulation." The subject seems to renounce it (as if it no longer figured in his corporeal schema). In the same way, language places a phoneme which it had previously used "out of circulation" without there being any question of a veritable convention or decision.

In the activity of the body, like that of language, there is a blind logic, since laws of equilibrium are observed by the community of speaking subjects without any of them being conscious of it. In opposition to this spontaneous logic, there is the voluntary logic of the phenomena of hyperurbanism and hyperdialectism.

2. In our consideration of grammar, we have seen that the word could be defined above all by its value as a tool, that it had a range rather than a *signification*. In French, the particle *ti* as it is still used by some of Molière's characters (*J'aime-ti pas ma fille?*) cannot be explained by a logical analysis. Originally, the interrogative form of the present indicative could be used for all persons. Then, gradually, it ceased to be used for the first two persons in the singular and plural (*aimons-nous, aimez-vous*) because it was equivocal with the reflexive, and it underwent a weakening in the first two persons of the singular for euphonic reasons. The form that was appropriate to the third person (*aime-t-il*) invaded the other persons; and *t-il* pronounced as *ti* came to signify the interrogative itself. Thus, one could say *j'aime-ti pas ma fille?* When considering this birth of a quasi-particle (*ti*) in French, we explain that it is not possible to give to the Greek particle "ἄν" an analysis which would reduce its different meanings to one.

Pronouns, genders, and numbers also tend toward a value according to how they are used. The meaning of a word ends up by being reduced to the consciousness of a possible substitution with some words but not with others. In particular, it has appeared to us that a logical analysis of the proposition is impossible.

It appears, then, that one would not know how to resolve the problem of language by conceiving it as a series of signs, each bearing a signification or a concept. In language, the consciousness of signification is not exhaustive; it does not go as far as a concept and, correlatively, it is less *behind* the sign than mixed up with it. It is like the halo of the sign's possible uses in communication. Every isolated word presupposes a present state of dialogue. Each sentence is the modulation of a total, commonly-held power of expression. Similarly, to know how to play the piano consists not of being able to execute some pieces but of having a general means of translating written notes into music. To know how to speak is not to have a finite number of pure signs and pure significations at one's disposal.

These remarks return us to certain ideas of Saussure that have guided the work of linguists in the whole contemporary period. Saussure admits that language is essentially *diacritic*: words do not carry meaning as much as they separate themselves out from others. This is to say that each linguistic phenomenon is a differentiation of a global movement of communication. In a language, Saussure says, all is negative; there are only differences, and no positive terms. The side of the signified [*signifié*] amounts to conceptual differences, the side of the signifier [*signifiant*] to phonic differences.

Thus, in speaking of language "value" (as one speaks of the value of a coin), rather than "signification," one ought to say that it can be exchanged for an infinite number of objects. There is a polysemy of the word as there is a plurality of possible usages of the same piece of money. Michel Bréal compares words with historical institutions.[15] For example, Parliament was originally a court of justice. It began with the right of recording royal edicts, but progressively acquired the right of remonstrance. In the eighteenth century, we find it at the point of becoming an organ of political opposition. Similarly, the word that has been introduced to signify one thing loses its original meaning and acquires another. At each moment, the meaning is an element of a total configuration. In this light, one can consider language as an aspect of what "cultural" sociologists call "culture." When

15. [See Michel Bréal, *Semantics: Studies on the Science of Meaning*, trans. Mrs. Henry Cust (London: Heinemann, 1900).]

Saussure speaks of the "conventional" character of language, he uses another vocabulary to express the idea that language is "cultural," not "natural."

B. [*Saussure's Views*]

1. Saussure's efforts with respect to language are double:

(*a*) On the one hand, there is a return to living spoken language: "language is not an entity; it exists only in speaking subjects."

Written language, placed under the custodianship of living language which is posterior to it, cannot give us the key to language. Nevertheless, it can sometimes obtain a rigor and an articulation of expression which spoken language does not have.

(*b*) But, at the same time, language is not a function of the speaking subject. Involved in the speaking community, the speaking subject is not the proprietor of his language. Language is wholly *the will to understand and to be understood.* Here Saussure encounters the principal philosophical problem of the relationship between the individual and the social.

For Saussure, the individual is neither the *subject* nor the *object* of history but both simultaneously. Thus language is not a transcendent reality with respect to all the speaking subjects; nor is it a phantasm formed by the individual. It is a manifestation of human intersubjectivity. Saussure elucidates the enigmatic relationship linking the individual to history by his analysis of language (one of the most fundamental social realities). He considers linguistics to be a part of a more general "semeiotic."

2. First, we will study the relationships which bind society through language. Then we will generalize and will attempt to sketch a general idea of the relationships between the individual and the collective.

(*a*) The relationships between sign and signification. Saussure starts off with the idea that *everything in language is psychological.* The contemporary word is not purely and simply the result in itself of words which have come about historically. One must distinguish between *substantial identity* (e.g., I can find the same coat that had been stolen from me at the second-hand clothing shop) and *structural identity* (e.g., the express at 9:17 is always the 9:17 express, even though it is neither the same train, nor the same engineer). Between the French word for "sea" [*mer*] and the original Latin word *mare,* there is not a substantial identity but rather a structural identity. There has been a continuous passage from one generation to another without any consciousness of word change. It is not the phonetic or material continuity which is the foundation of the word's identity; on the contrary, the continuity presupposes the identity.

As far as *forms* are concerned, there is no reason to *explain* contemporary French by the French of the eighteenth century. For example: the expression "good buy" [*bon marché*] must be considered today as a unique attribute. It is the value of a word which accounts for its identity, just as a chess piece defines itself not by its matter, but by certain possibilities of defense and offense. This indicates to what extent everything is mental [*psychique*] within a language.

But here what is mental is not individual. In effect, a language is not a nomenclature, a sum of signs attached to a certain number of significations. Words are interdependent systems of power with respect to one another. Nowhere can one confront *a* word and *its* signification. There is no relationship except between the verbal chain and the signified universe. Within the same language, all the signs which express the same ideas limit one another.

For example, the area of action for the word *mouton* is not the same in French as that of "mutton" in English, because English possesses two words, of which one ("sheep") serves to designate the animal and the other ("mutton") designates the meat.

As another example, in certain languages, there are two words for designating the sun, according to whether one speaks of the sun in itself or of its radiance toward earth.

The most exact characteristic of a word is "what the others are not." Signification exists not for a word but for all words in relation to one another. Our present tense could never be the same as the present tense of a language without a future tense.

It is for this reason that one can never exactly translate from one language into another. Thus the linguistic phenomenon is this coexistence of a multiplicity of signs. These signs have no meaning when taken individually but can be defined from a totality for which they themselves are the constituents. There are only "conceptual differences" and phonetic "differences" (Saussure). Thus, our ordinary manner of considering language in its relations with consciousness is false. Language in its functioning transcends the habitual distinction of pure meaning and pure sign.

At that point, each speaking subject finds himself reintegrated into the collectivity of speaking subjects. It is the *global will* to communicate with the alter ego that founds the positive [aspect] of the linguistic phenomenon. But this linguistic phenomenon, considered instant by instant, is never anything but negative, diacritic. It is the currency for a global possibility of communicating which makes up the very essence of the speaking subject.

(*b*) The relationship between the speaking subject and the expressive system. One cannot absolutely distinguish language from the speaking subject. Thought without words is like a "puff of air." Inversely, words without thought are no more than a chaos of sonorous signs. The function of language is to reveal thought, which is articulated at the intersection of these two chaotic [systems]; the function of language is not to serve as a material means for the expression of thought. "Pure thought," says Saussure, is like the puff of wind without shape or contour. Language in itself is like masses of water in a lake which has no configuration. Thought is articulated and determined at the point of contact of these two amorphous realities, at the surface of the water, which produces the waves, their geometric forms, their facets. There is "neither a materialization of thought, nor a spiritualization of language"; language and thought are only two moments of one and the same reality.

This leads to an original conception of the relationship between mind and object.

(*c*) The relationship between reason and chance.

i. The speech-language distinction. Speech [*parole*] is what one says; language [*langue*] is the treasure out of which the subject draws in order to speak; it is a system of possibilities.

But how can one arrive at this French "in itself"? In reality, each time that I speak, I allude to my language as a totality. It is difficult for me to delimit the frontiers of speech and of language. The distinction cannot maintain itself under such a simple form.

ii. The diachronic-synchronic distinction. From the diachronic point of view, language is considered in the succession of time, according to a longitudinal slice. It appears as a series of accidental events. In the decline of a system which has fallen into disuse, we can detect the accidental utilization of a detail which will be taken up later and systematized.

From the synchronic point of view, language is considered in its totality at a moment of its becoming; it reveals itself as tending toward a certain order, as forming a system.

Let us imagine that a planet is suddenly eliminated; the whole planetary system will be modified as a result. It will reorganize itself according to the utilization of the forces that inhabit it. The same is true in linguistics. Chance is at the basis of all the restructurings of language. In this sense, one can say that language is the domain of the *relatively motivated:* nothing rational can be found therein unless it is derived from some mode of chance which has been taken up and elaborated as the means of systematic expression by the community of speaking subjects.

One could revise certain Saussurian conceptions of the relation between the synchronic and the diachronic. G. Guillaume posits the existence of a sublinguistic scheme; it is defined by an architechtonic, in its different modes of expression, which develops through time and which guides the diachronic. Therefore, language would not be a *Gestalt* of the moment, but a *Gestalt* in movement, evolving toward a certain equilibrium. Moreover, the *Gestalt* would be capable of losing this equilibrium, once it has been obtained, by a phenomenon of wearing down and of seeking a new equilibrium in another direction. According to a conception of this sort, there is therefore an internal principle to language which selects from the accidents of the diachronic. Here chance and reason, diachronic and synchronic, are no longer simply *juxtaposed* as in Saussure.

But even with those, like G. Guillaume, who rework the Saussurian conception of the relationship between synchronic and diachronic, an essential element of Saussure's thought remains: the idea of a kind of blundering logic, in which the development is not guaranteed. This logic can bear all kinds of diversions. Nevertheless, order and system are reestablished by the thrust of speaking subjects who want to understand and be understood.

C. *Application to the Philosophy of History*

The Saussurian conception, if generalized, would perhaps permit one to find a road between the two major attitudes in the philosophy of history: (*a*) *history* is the sum of independent *chance* events (e.g., the nose of Cleopatra); (*b*) *history is providential;* it is a manifestation of an internal structure; it is a development that can be understood.

Bossuet's (*Discours sur l'histoire universelle*) and Hegel's (*The Philosophy of History*) conceptions of history both allow for historical destiny: the mind leads the world and historical reason works "behind the back of individuals." [16] In fact, this appears as a retrospective rationalization (Bergson, Aron). It is an afterthought that the idea appears to be a causal one; this is because its conditions of realization are by given hypotheses. The meaning and the orientation of history are never realizable at the present moment without the competition of present events. These events occur in the nick of time by such and such an individual who is an exceptional "midwife" (Lenin) of events, etc. No power could *absolutely* guarantee the expiration of these events, even if it were rendered *probable.*

What Saussure saw is precisely this masking of chance and order, this return to the rational, the fortuitous. One could apply his conception of the history of language to history as a whole. The driving force of language is the will to communicate ("we are thrown into language" [*langue*], situated in language

16. [Jacques-Bénigne Bossuet, *Discours sur l'histoire universelle* (Paris: Garnier Frères, 1873). G. W. F. Hegel, *The Philosophy of History*, trans. J. Sibree (New York: Dover, 1900).]

[*langage*], and engaged by it [*langage*] in a process of rational explanation with other people). Similarly that which moves the whole historical development is the *common situation* of men, their will to coexist and to recognize one another.

The principle of order and of historical rationality does not eliminate chance. It turns chance or uses chance. As Saussure might say, it converts the accidental into systems. It solicits and surrounds the pure event without eliminating it. Perhaps it is an idea of this sort which allows for the originality of the *Marxist* conception of history (in opposition to the Hegelian system). At least, Trotsky understood it this way when he said that the logic of history can be considered through metaphors, as a kind of "natural selection" (certainly this is not anything but a metaphor; the forces that are at play here are those of human productivity and not of nature; that is, it is rather a question of "historical selection"). If certain regimes disappear, it is because they are incapable of resolving the problems of time and the intersubjective force of the moment. That which we call the logic of history is a process of elimination by which only the systems which are capable of taking the situation into account subsist. History is not a hidden god which acts in our place and to which we must submit. Men make their history as they make their language.

D. *Conclusion*

One could say about language in its relations with thought what one says of the life of the body in its relations with consciousness. Just as one could not place the body at the first level, just as one could not subordinate it or draw it out of its autonomy (S. de Beauvoir), one can say only that language makes thought, as much as it is made by thought. Thought inhabits language and language is its body. This mediation of the objective and of the subjective, of the interior and of the exterior—what philosophy seeks to do—we can find in language if we succeed in getting close enough to it.

Index